Paul Bradshaw is Professor of Liturgy at the University of Notre Dame, USA, an honorary canon of the Episcopal Diocese of Northern Indiana, a priest-vicar of Westminster Abbey and a member of the Church of England Liturgical Commission. A former president of the North American Academy of Liturgy and of the international Societas Liturgica, as well as editor-in-chief of the journal *Studia Liturgica* from 1987 to 2005, he has written or edited over 20 books. Among them are *The Search for the Origins of Christian Worship* (2nd edn, SPCK, London/OUP, New York 2002) and *Reconstructing Early Christian Worship* (SPCK, London 2009).

D0289949

EARLY CHRISTIAN WORSHIP

A Basic Introduction to Ideas and Practice

Second Edition

PAUL F. BRADSHAW

LITURGICAL PRESS
Collegeville, Minnesota

www.litpress.org

Published in 2010 for the United States and Canada by
LITURGICAL PRESS
Collegeville, Minnesota 56321

First published in 1996 by the Society for Promoting Christian Knowledge. Second edition published in 2010.

7 8 9

ISBN 978-0-8146-3366-3

Contents

Acknowledgements and abbreviations   vi
Introduction   vii

Part 1
CHRISTIAN INITIATION

1 Beginnings   3
2 Syria and Egypt   9
3 Rome and North Africa   15
4 The fourth-century synthesis   23
5 From adult to infant baptism   33

Part 2
EUCHARIST

6 Sacred meal   41
7 Anamnesis and epiclesis: the eucharistic prayer   49
8 Holy food   56
9 'The bloodless sacrifice'   62
10 'Let all mortal flesh keep silence'   70

Part 3
LITURGICAL TIME

11 Daily prayer   77
12 Sunday   83
13 Easter and Pentecost   88
14 Christmas, Epiphany and Lent   94
15 Saints' days   99

Index   102

Acknowledgements and abbreviations

Where some of the following translations of ancient writings use non-inclusive language with regard to human beings, they have been amended in the extracts cited in this book. Any translations not otherwise attributed are the work of the author.

AIR Edward Yarnold, *The Awe-Inspiring Rites of Initiation*, 2nd edition. Copyright 1994 T & T Clark, Edinburgh.

DBL E. C. Whitaker, ed., *Documents of the Baptismal Liturgy*, revised and expanded by Maxwell E. Johnson. Copyright 2003 SPCK, London. Extracts reprinted with permission.

PEER R. C. D. Jasper and G. J. Cuming, eds, *Prayers of the Eucharist: Early and Reformed*, 3rd edition. Copyright 1987 by The Order of Saint Benedict, Inc. Published by Liturgical Press, Collegeville, Minnesota. Reprinted with permission.

Introduction

It is a sign of the extent of the continuing research that has taken place into the history of early Christian worship by myself and others in the 15 years since I originally wrote this book that scarcely any chapter has been left unchanged in this revised edition. Although in some cases the adjustments have been relatively minor, in others extensive rewriting has had to be done, so differently do many scholars now interpret the evidence that was presented there.

Originally commissioned as an undergraduate textbook for the University of South Africa and then offered to a wider audience, this little work aims not merely to describe *what* rites Christians performed during the first few centuries of the Church's existence but also to explain *why* they did them: What caused them to choose those particular liturgical forms instead of others? What did they understand themselves to be doing in their worship? What effect did that have on the development of Christian doctrine? And how did new doctrinal formulations in turn affect the character of the rites? If readers keep these questions in mind as they go through each chapter, they should have little difficulty in finding the answers in the text.

In such a small volume it has not been possible to deal with the subject in great detail, but suggestions are included for further reading for those who wish to go further, and more extensive background to the sources and methods used in the study of early Christian liturgy can be found in the second edition of my book, *The Search for the Origins of Christian Worship* (SPCK, London, and Oxford University Press, New York 2002).

Paul Bradshaw

Part 1

CHRISTIAN INITIATION

In this section we shall first examine the roots of Christian baptismal thought and practice in New Testament times, and then see how different elements of this were picked up and developed in various early Christian traditions, concentrating principally on the contrasts between Syria and North Africa, before going on to look at the movement towards a more common baptismal theology and liturgy in the fourth century. We shall end our survey by considering the effects that the later spread of infant baptism had on both the practice and understanding of Christian initiation.

Suggestions for further reading

In addition to works cited in notes, the following are recommended:

Paul F. Bradshaw, *Reconstructing Early Christian Worship* (SPCK, London 2009), chapters 4–6.

Maxwell E. Johnson, *The Rites of Christian Initiation* (2nd edn, Liturgical Press, Collegeville 2007), chapters 1–5.

Bryan D. Spinks, *Early and Medieval Rituals and Theologies of Baptism* (Ashgate, Aldershot 2006), chapters 1–3.

1

Beginnings

Jesus apparently did not leave his followers with a fixed set of doctrines but rather with an experience that changed their lives, which they then tried to articulate in their own ways. As a result, what we find in the New Testament is not one standard theology of baptism or a systematized explanation of what it means to become a Christian, but a variety of ways of speaking about that experience, quite different images and metaphors being employed by different writers in their attempts to communicate it to others.

Antecedents

The New Testament implies that the custom of baptizing those who were converted to the Christian faith was derived from John the Baptist (see, for example, Matthew 3.1–12), but the source of his own practice is uncertain. Some scholars have argued that it was based on the ablutions of the Jewish Essene community at Qumran, but these were repeated washings related to the need for constant ritual purity and do not seem to have included an initiatory baptism. Others have suggested that John was influenced by the practice of baptizing new converts to Judaism, but there is some doubt whether this was being done in his time or whether it was only adopted at a later date. A third possibility is that it arose out of the Israelite traditions of ritual purification (see, for example, Leviticus 15.5–13) and/or of prophetic symbolism, which had spoken of God's people being cleansed with pure water in preparation for the advent of the messianic age (see, for example, Ezekiel 36.2–8).

Whether the Christian adoption of baptism began with Jesus himself or only in the Church after his resurrection cannot easily be resolved. All three synoptic Gospels record Jesus' own baptism by John but say nothing of him baptizing his followers. The Gospel of John, on the other hand, does not mention Jesus being baptized but does speak of him baptizing others (John 3.22, 26; 4.1; but cf. 4.2). Matthew 28.19–20 contains a command to baptize all nations, but there are difficulties in accepting this as an authentic saying of the risen Lord.

Baptismal practice

Whatever its origins, however, it appears that at least in certain Christian communities from early times it became the custom to initiate new converts into the Church through a process which included baptism in water. Unfortunately, the New Testament offers very few clues as to the manner in which the baptisms might have been carried out. The preference for the use of 'living' (i.e. naturally flowing) water that is found in some later sources (see also John 7.38) suggests that they may at first have usually been performed in a river or pool, where possible, rather than in a domestic bath-house. The image of baptism as participation in the death and resurrection of Christ used by Paul (see Romans 6.3ff.) seems naturally to imply that candidates would have been totally submerged in the water, but such a practice would certainly not have been easily possible in domestic baths, and the custom found later in some places of candidates standing in a shallow font and having water poured all over them may also have existed in the earliest times. Both methods involved total immersion in water – it was only the way of achieving it that differed.

What else besides the actual immersion might have been involved is not made explicit in the New Testament. We would expect there to have been a preliminary period of instruction in the faith, at least in the case of Gentile candidates who lacked the religious background possessed by Jewish converts, but this need not have been the extensive formal catechumenate (from the Greek word *catechumen*, 'learner') found in later centuries. Several New Testament passages speak of baptism being 'in the name of Jesus' (see, for example, Acts 2.38), which suggests that his name was invoked in some way during the ceremony. This could have been in the form of a statement made over the candidate (e.g. 'I baptize you in the name of . . .'), such as we find in later Syrian usage, but it need not necessarily have been restricted to that. It could also have referred to some confession of faith in Jesus made by the candidate at the moment of baptism, such as we find in later Western sources. At the very least, it seems probable that some sort of ritual dialogue would have preceded the immersion. Acts 2.38 refers to the necessity for repentance to accompany baptism, and this would surely have needed to be expressed verbally. Similarly, Acts 8.37, although found only in certain manuscripts of the text, seems to embody the sort of profession of faith that candidates in some places would have made prior to baptism: 'I believe that Jesus Christ is the Son of God.'

'Confirmation' in the New Testament?

Some scholars have argued that in New Testament times the immersion in water was regularly followed within the same ceremony by a separate ritual gesture expressing the gift of the Holy Spirit, either in the form of the imposition of hands on the newly baptized or by an anointing with oil, and that this constitutes the biblical foundation of the later practice of 'confirmation'. They point to such passages as Matthew 3.16, Mark 1.10, and Luke 3.22, where Jesus receives the Holy Spirit immediately after his baptism; to Acts 8.14–17, where Peter and John lay their hands on the Samaritans baptized by Philip and they receive the Holy Spirit; to Acts 19.1–7, where baptism is followed by the imposition of Paul's hands and the reception of the Holy Spirit; to Hebrews 6.2, which mentions 'the laying on of hands' directly after 'ablutions'; to 2 Corinthians 1.22, Ephesians 1.13 and 4.30, where Christians are spoken of as having been sealed with the Holy Spirit; to Revelation 7.3, which speaks of the servants of God being sealed upon their foreheads; and to 1 John 2.20 and 27, which refer to an anointing by the Holy One that the readers have received.

Other scholars, however, have contested this interpretation of the passages. They argue that the descriptions of Jesus' baptism do not necessarily mirror the ritual structure of early Christian baptisms, and the two narratives in Acts may not describe the regular form of Christian initiation but instead be accounts of unusual situations: the mission of the Hellenists in Samaria had to be endorsed by the Jerusalem apostles, and the disciples of John needed baptism in the name of Jesus in order to receive the gift of the Holy Spirit. We need to remember that Acts also describes the gift of the Spirit as preceding the act of immersion in the case of the baptism of the household of Cornelius (Acts 10.44–48). Since this episode is usually interpreted as being an exceptional situation, symbolizing a Gentile equivalent of the Pentecost experience (Acts 2.1–4), rather than a description of standard initiatory practice, why should the same not be true of the other baptismal accounts? As for the other New Testament references cited above, that in Hebrews is too vague to allow any firm conclusions to be drawn about baptismal practice, and the various allusions to 'sealing' and 'anointing' may not be reflections of actual liturgical ceremonies but instead merely vivid metaphors for what was thought to have happened inwardly to those who became Christians.

Thus, at best, the New Testament evidence is inconclusive with regard to any post-baptismal ceremonies. Moreover, the theory that the imposition of hands was a standard element in first-century practice becomes still less credible when we take into account the testimony of the later liturgical traditions. As we shall see in subsequent chapters, while North African and Roman sources certainly do seem to have known a post-baptismal anointing and imposition of hands, the early Syrian practice apparently did not include any post-baptismal ceremonies at all, although it was familiar with a pre-baptismal anointing. This later diversity suggests that the whole idea of the existence of a uniform baptismal ritual in primitive Christianity is misconceived. While it is possible that some communities may have practised an anointing and/or imposition of hands from early times, it does not look as if all followed that custom, still less that there was some apostolic directive so to do – or else we would be at a loss to explain the subsequent Syrian departure from that norm. We cannot even say with total certainty that immersion in water was the one universal element in Christian initiation rites from the beginning. Again, it is possible that immersion was originally limited only to certain groups, with others perhaps having different practices, some of which – such as anointing or foot-washing – may have survived as ancillary rites to water baptism in the more standardized initiation process of later centuries.

Baptismal images and metaphors

The language and images used about baptism by the New Testament writers further support the idea that there were variations in liturgical practice from place to place. For what we find here is not a standardized baptismal theology shared by all Christians but a range of different ways of interpreting and expressing what was thought to happen when a person became a Christian. Hebrews 6.4 and 10.32, for instance, speaks of the baptized as having been 'illuminated'. The same image underlies the statement in 1 Peter 2.9 that God has 'called you out of darkness into his marvellous light'; and it recurs, as we shall see in a later chapter, in the description of baptism in the second-century writer Justin Martyr. John 3, on the other hand, uses instead the metaphor of rebirth by water and Spirit; a similar concept also appears in Titus 3.5, which speaks of 'the washing of regeneration and renewal in the Holy Spirit'; and once again this idea is picked up by Justin Martyr. In the Acts of the Apostles, the emphasis falls instead on the forgiveness of sins and the gift of the Holy Spirit, as, for example, in Acts 2.38: 'And Peter said to them, "Repent, and be baptized every one of you in the name of Jesus Christ for the forgiveness of your sins; and you shall receive the gift of the Holy Spirit."'

By contrast to these ways of speaking, in Paul's baptismal theology the primary image seems to have been union with Christ through participation in his death and resurrection (see especially Romans 6.2ff.; Colossians 2.12). But he also makes use of other metaphors. As I have mentioned earlier, he speaks of Christians as having been sealed as God's people: '[God] has put his seal upon us and given us his Spirit in our hearts as a guarantee' (2 Corinthians 1.22). The same image recurs in the Epistle to the Ephesians, where the readers are said to have been 'sealed with the promised Holy Spirit, which is the guarantee of our inheritance' (1.13–14; see also 4.30); and a similar theme is found in Revelation 7.30, which speaks of the servants of God being sealed upon their foreheads. This metaphor seems to be derived from commerce, where a seal authenticated a change of ownership: Christians were once slaves to sin, but now they have been marked as belonging instead to God (see Romans 6.16–23), and the Holy Spirit constitutes, as it were, the 'deposit' which guarantees that the transaction will be brought to completion when Christ returns.

Galatians 3.27 offers what seems to be yet another metaphorical image, that of baptism as being clothed in a new garment, since it describes the baptized as having 'put on Christ'; and Colossians 3.9–10 and Ephesians 4.22–24 speak of putting off the old nature and putting on the new. There is also a similar eschatological picture in 2 Corinthians 5.2–3, which talks of the longing 'to put on our heavenly dwelling, so that . . . we may not be found naked'. Such language may well have arisen as a result of baptismal candidates stripping off their clothes and going down naked into the water and then dressing again when they emerged from it. Although we have no first-century testimony that this was then the usual practice, it is well attested in later sources. To these citations, we may perhaps add the references in Mark's Gospel to the young man at the arrest of Jesus who left the linen cloth he was wearing and ran away naked (14.51–52) and of the young man sitting on the right side of the empty tomb, dressed in a white robe (16.5). It has been suggested by some that this pair of stories was intended as a baptismal image, and that is certainly an attractive interpretation of passages which have often puzzled commentators. It is interesting to observe that fourth-century sources speak of the newly baptized not just putting back on their former garments, but being clothed in white robes. Could this practice possibly go back to New Testament times, or is it – as seems more likely – a much later development that was encouraged by such texts as Revelation 7.9–14, which describes the countless multitude wearing robes washed white in the blood of the Lamb?

Finally, we should note that the image of being 'anointed' with the Holy Spirit found in 1 John 2.20 and 27 arose out of a different concept from that of being 'sealed' with the Spirit used in the Pauline writings. In Israelite tradition both kings and priests had been anointed when they were appointed, as a sign that they had been chosen by God. For example, in 1 Samuel 16.1–13 the prophet Samuel anoints David as king 'and the Spirit of the Lord came mightily upon David from that day forward' (v. 13). The term 'Messiah' itself means in Hebrew 'the anointed one', which was translated into Greek as *Christos*, Christ; and so it is hardly surprising that early Christian writers thought of Jesus as having been anointed by God with the Holy Spirit (see Luke 4.16; Acts 4.27; Acts 10.38) or at least as having received God's Spirit at his baptism (Matthew 3.16; Mark 1.10; Luke 3.22). Since they believed that Christians at their baptism received the same Holy Spirit, it was but a small step to think that they, too, were being anointed as Jesus had been. The idea that Christians constituted a 'royal priesthood' (1 Peter 2.9; see also 2.5) or a kingdom of priests (cf. Revelation 1.6; see also 5.10), which was derived from Exodus 19.6, would also have contributed to seeing baptism as anointing. Both these images led quite naturally to the adoption of a literal anointing with oil as a baptismal ceremony, such as we find in later sources.

2

Syria and Egypt

Syria

Our sources of information for baptismal practice in the early Syrian tradition are rather sparse, but enough to enable us to piece together a rough outline of how Christian initiation was performed and understood there in the second and third centuries.

The *Didache*

Chapter 7 of the ancient church order known as the *Didache*, or 'Teaching of the Twelve Apostles', paints a very simple picture:

> Concerning baptism, baptize thus: having first recounted all these things, baptize in the name of the Father and of the Son and of the Holy Spirit in living water; if you do not have living water, baptize in other water; if you cannot in cold, then in warm; if you do not have either, pour water three times on the head in the name of Father, Son, and Holy Spirit. Before the baptism let the baptizer and the one to be baptized and any others who can fast; you shall instruct the one to be baptized to fast one or two [days] before.

Scholars have found it difficult to date the *Didache* precisely, but usually place its compilation somewhere between the second half of the first century and the first half of the second century. These instructions suggest that the normal pattern of Christian initiation consisted of a period of instruction and fasting, by both candidate and at least some members of the Christian community, followed by immersion in running water accompanied by the recitation of the name of the Trinity. This trinitarian formula may be a later addition to the text and the original version may have simply been baptism in the name of the Lord.[1] Nevertheless, the formula is reminiscent

---

[1] There is also a passage in the apocryphal *Acts of Paul* where Thecla immerses herself in water, saying, 'In the name of Jesus Christ I baptize myself...', which

of Matthew 28.19–20 ('Go therefore and make disciples of all nations, baptizing them in the name of the Father and of the Son and of the Holy Spirit, teaching them to observe all that I have commanded you'); and whenever they were written, both passages imply that the earliest custom of invoking the name of Jesus in baptism was eventually expanded in this way, as the Church began to define its faith more fully. Other sources confirm what was intended by these references was that the one baptizing should say over the candidate: 'I baptize you in the name of the Father and of the Son and of the Holy Spirit.'

The main concern of the baptismal instructions in the *Didache*, however, is to make provision for occasions when it was impossible to perform the ritual in what was seen as the normal way: immersion in cold, running water. Again, this suggests the Church was undergoing a transition from an outdoor, missionary context to a more domestic situation that required some modification of its earlier practices.

The *Didascalia*

When we compare these simple directions with other early Syrian sources, however, the most striking feature is the important place that they give to a pre-baptismal anointing with oil. The third-century Syrian church order known as the *Didascalia Apostolorum*, for example, requires female deacons to be appointed in order to carry out this ministry for women candidates, and it instructs the bishop as follows:

> In the first place, when women go down into the baptismal water: those who go down into the water ought to be anointed by a deaconess with the oil of anointing; and where there is no woman to hand, and especially no deaconess, he who baptizes must of necessity anoint the woman who is being baptized. But where there is a woman, and especially a deaconess, present, it is not fitting that women should be seen by men, but with the imposition of the hand you should anoint the head only. As of old priests and kings were anointed in Israel, so do you likewise, with the imposition of the hand, anoint the head of those who receive baptism, whether it be of men or of women; and afterwards, whether you yourself baptize, or you tell the deacons

---

seems to point to a formula something like 'I baptize you in the name of Jesus Christ' as having been usual in early times. See J. K. Elliott, *The Apocryphal New Testament* (Clarendon, Oxford 1993), p. 370.

or presbyters to baptize, let a woman, a deaconess, anoint the women, as we have already said. But let a man pronounce over them the invocation of the divine names in the water.[2]

The *Didascalia* regards the pre-baptismal unction of the candidates' heads performed by the imposition of the bishop's hand not only as an expression of their entry into the royal priesthood of the Church (see 1 Peter 2.5 and 9; Revelation 1.6; 5.10), but as reflecting Christ's own baptism, for it says elsewhere that 'the Lord in baptism, by the imposition of hand of the bishop, bore witness to each one of you and uttered his holy voice, saying: "Thou art my son: this day have I begotten thee"' (Psalm 2.7/Luke 3.22).[3] However, it seems that it also expected that their whole bodies would be anointed as well: otherwise, there would have been no necessity for the female deacons.

The *Acts of Thomas*

We come across this same twofold unction in other Syrian texts from the same period. The third-century apocryphal *Acts of Thomas* contains several descriptions of baptisms. Two refer to an anointing of the head alone before the immersion and associate this with the Messiah (chs 27 and 132). Two others include a prayer for the blessing of the oil, mention the anointing of both the head and the whole body, and associate the action instead with healing (chs 121 and 157). A fifth account speaks explicitly only of the immersion in water, at least in the Syriac version of the text, although an allusion to the 'seal' here could be an oblique reference to anointing (ch. 49).

While it is possible to harmonize these various accounts of anointing by surmising that an unction of both head and body was presumed in every case, but only explicitly mentioned in two of them, the scholar Gabriele Winkler put forward the theory that they represent two different stages of development in the baptismal rite: the earlier practice was to anoint the head alone, as continued to be the custom in the later Armenian rite, and the anointing of the whole body was a later addition to the ritual. This explained why at first oil was poured over the head alone (this was the custom at the anointing of the kings of Israel), why the coming of the Spirit was associated with it (the Spirit

---

[2] *Didascalia* 3.12; English translation from Sebastian Brock and Michael Vasey, *The Liturgical Portions of the Didascalia* (Grove Books, Nottingham 1982), p. 22.
[3] *Didascalia* 2.32.

of the Lord came over the newly nominated king), and why it was the anointing and not the immersion in water that seemed to be regarded as the central feature of baptism in the early Syrian sources (this was the only visible gesture for what was held to be the central event at Christ's baptism – his revelation as the Messiah-King through the descent of the Spirit). The later introduction of the anointing of the whole body would thus have led to a reinterpretation of the significance of the oil in terms of a healing of the whole person, and hence to the addition of prayers that sanctified the oil and invested it with healing power.[4]

However, what we have here may be not so much different stages in the evolution of the rites as reflections of variant local traditions. Some Christian communities in Syria certainly appear to have adopted an anointing of the head alone as a symbol of participation in the spirit of the Messiah, as we have evidence of this as a continuing practice not only in Armenia but also in some later Syrian sources.[5] Others may have practised instead an anointing of the whole head and body as a symbol of protection and healing, perhaps influenced by pagan religions; and still other groups may have known only the immersion in water, as seems to be the case in the *Didache*. It is even possible that at least some of those for whom the anointing was the central feature of initiation may not at first have included a water baptism at all in their practice. Thus, only gradually would these Syrian Christians have appropriated elements and concepts from one another's traditions into their own. This might help to explain why even when the anointing of the head is understood to confer the Spirit, it precedes rather than follows the water bath, in contrast to the sequence of the gospel accounts of Jesus' baptism, and why in other cases, including the *Didascalia*, the Spirit is understood to be conferred through immersion in the water rather than by the preceding anointing of head and body.[6]

---

[4] 'The Original Meaning of the Prebaptismal Anointing and its Implications', *Worship* 52 (1978), pp. 24–45; reprinted in Maxwell E. Johnson (ed.), *Living Water, Sealing Spirit* (Liturgical Press, Collegeville 1995), pp. 58–81.

[5] See Sebastian Brock, 'Studies in the Early History of the Syrian Orthodox Baptismal Liturgy', *Journal of Theological Studies* 23 (1972), pp. 16–64, here at pp. 21, 30 (especially n. 2), 39; idem, 'Some Early Syrian Baptismal Commentaries', *Orientalia Christiana Periodica* 46 (1980), pp. 20–61.

[6] See *Didascalia* 2.41, where it is said that someone who has committed serious sin and repents should be reconciled by the imposition of the hand: 'For him the

Faith and baptism

The Syrian sources also reveal another distinctive feature in their initiation practice, a two-stage ritual. The *Didascalia* offers the first sign of this in its statement that 'when the heathen desire and promise to repent, saying "We believe", we receive them into the congregation so that they may hear the word, but do not receive them into communion until they receive the seal and are fully initiated'.[7] It may seem odd that converts were expected to express their repentance and faith *before* they were allowed to hear the word, but probably what is meant here is that, while there would have been some preliminary instruction primarily of an ethical kind designed to bring them to repentance and faith, certain teachings were reserved until after they had made an expression of commitment to Christ. Although the teaching had apparently been removed from this interval in the fourth century, John Chrysostom seems to have known at Antioch both a formula of renunciation of evil and an act of adherence to Christ ('I pledge myself to you, O Christ') still occurring on the day before the baptism. A similar pattern can also be found in the rite of Constantinople in the fifth century; and the testimony of Theodore of Mopsuestia (fourth century) and the later Syrian rites show traces of this twofold structure, even though both parts now take place on the same occasion.

Egypt

The complete pattern of the earliest baptismal practice in Egypt is not easy to discern because of a lack of evidence, but certain features can be made out. In some respects there are resemblances to Syrian practice. In particular, like the Syrian rites, the Egyptian tradition seems at first to have known only a pre-baptismal anointing and no post-baptismal ceremonies. The meaning attached to this anointing is not very fully spelled out, but it is clearly considered integral to the baptism, is certainly not exorcistic in character, and appears to have been accompanied

---

imposition of the hand shall take the place of baptism: for whether it be by the imposition of the hand, or by baptism, they then receive the communion of the Holy Spirit' (Brock and Vasey, *Liturgical Portions of the Didascalia*, p. 13); and later John Chrysostom, *Baptismal Homily* 2.25–6 (*DBL*, p. 46).

[7] 2.39 (Brock and Vasey, *Liturgical Portions of the Didascalia*, p. 12).

by a trinitarian formula, which we also find in fourth-century Syrian sources. A prayer over the oil in the fourth-century *Sacramentary of Sarapion* speaks of its function in terms of healing and re-creation; Cyril of Alexandria (d. 444) termed it the 'chrism of catechesis'; and the later Coptic rites call it 'the oil of gladness' – a designation also used by John Chrysostom in Antioch. On the other hand, in at least two respects Egyptian practice was different from the Syrian.

The baptismal season

It became the custom in Egypt for Christians to observe a 40-day season of fasting in imitation of Jesus' fast in the wilderness, probably immediately after Epiphany (see below, pp. 97–8). Because, as in other parts of the world, baptism was usually preceded by a period of fasting by both candidates and community, the end of this season seems to have been adopted as the preferred time of year for baptisms to take place, with the 40 days then constituting the period of the catechumenate. The candidates were apparently enrolled at the beginning of that season, received instruction and fasted together with the Christian community during it, and underwent a final scrutiny as to their readiness for admission to baptism two days before the end of it and the time for the administration of the baptismal rite. When in the fourth century this Lenten season was taken over more widely in Christianity and placed immediately prior to Easter, it led to the 40 days also being adopted as the period of baptismal preparation in those places too.

The profession of faith

In another respect, Egyptian baptismal practice seems to have resembled Western rather than Eastern custom. It appears from third-century sources that the immersion in water was accompanied or preceded by creedal interrogation similar to that found in North Africa and at Rome (in which the candidates responded to questions about their belief in the Trinity), rather than by an affirmation of faith of the kind revealed in Syrian sources, where the candidates themselves made a statement professing their adherence to Christ prior to the baptismal event. However, there are some signs that the fivefold confession of faith found instead of this interrogatory form in later Coptic liturgical rites may have also existed in early times, perhaps as an alternative to it in some places.

3

Rome and North Africa

Rome

Justin Martyr

Our earliest evidence comes from Justin Martyr, writing in the middle of the second century. He describes baptism thus:

> Those who are convinced and believe what we say and teach is the truth, and pledge themselves to be able to live accordingly, are taught in prayer and fasting to ask God to forgive their past sins, while we pray and fast with them. Then we lead them to a place where there is water, and they are regenerated in the same manner in which we ourselves were regenerated. In the name of God, the Father and Lord of all, and of our Saviour, Jesus Christ, and of the Holy Spirit they then receive the washing with water . . . There is invoked over the one who wishes to be regenerated, and who is repentant of his sins, the name of God, the Father and Lord of all. This name only is invoked by him that leads to the washing him that is to be washed: for no one can speak the name of God, who is ineffable; and anyone who might boldly claim to do so is quite mad. This washing is called illumination, since they who learn these things are illuminated intellectually. Furthermore, the illuminated one is also baptized in the name of Jesus Christ, who was crucified under Pontius Pilate, and in the name of the Holy Spirit, who predicted through the prophets everything concerning Jesus.
>
> After thus baptizing those who have believed and given their assent, we escort them to the place where are assembled those whom we call brothers and sisters, to offer up sincere prayers in common for ourselves, for the newly baptized, and for all other persons wherever they may be . . . At the conclusion of prayers we greet one another with a kiss. Then, bread and cup containing water and wine mixed with water are presented to the one presiding over the brothers and sisters . . .[1]

---

[1] *First Apology* 61, 65; English translation from *DBL*, p. 3 (with minor additions).

15

The process thus appears relatively simple, consisting of a period (of unspecified duration) of instruction, fasting, and prayer, by both candidate and community before the baptism; then immersion itself, accompanied in some way by the invocation of the Trinity; and finally the entry into the assembly of other Christians to share in common prayer, the kiss, and the celebration of the Eucharist with them. Justin's description sounds very similar to what we have seen in Syria, and we need to remember that he himself was Syrian in origin and had been baptized at Ephesus, and so would have belonged to a community at Rome that was primarily Eastern in membership and probably followed Eastern liturgical customs. Thus what he provides is likely to be less of a description of *the* Roman liturgy than of one of a number of diverse traditions from different, largely ethnic, Christian groups in the city.

A small number of earlier scholars tried to argue that if one reads between the lines of Justin's writings, it is possible to discern there evidence suggesting that Justin did not regard water baptism as the whole of Christian initiation, but also knew of a post-baptismal ceremony that effected the gift of the Holy Spirit. Their arguments have, however, failed to convince many. On the other hand, somewhat better evidence for such a ceremony is provided in a letter by the third-century bishop of Rome Cornelius, that is quoted by the fourth-century church historian Eusebius, where he spoke of the heretic Novatian, after receiving emergency baptism while he was ill, having failed subsequently to receive the 'sealing' by the bishop, and continued: 'As he did not receive this, how could he receive the Holy Spirit?'[2] Although what this ritual 'sealing' consisted of is not explained, it could well have been an imposition of hands, especially as this seems to have been the contemporary tradition in North Africa, and Rome and North Africa tended to have many liturgical traditions in common.

It is interesting to note the images used by Justin to describe the meaning of the ritual: the New Testament ideas of rebirth, washing and illumination predominate; but there is no hint of the Pauline notion of participation in the death and resurrection of Christ. One might easily suppose that Justin omitted this simply because it would not have been easily intelligible to a pagan audience, but

---

[2] Eusebius, *Historia ecclesiastica* 6.43.20.

in fact hardly any Christian writer before the fourth century draws on that Pauline concept in connection with baptism. Hence, it seems as if it was not yet used as the central interpretation of the meaning of baptism that it was to become in later times.

The *Apostolic Tradition*

Many scholars would add to the apparent Roman evidence provided by Justin Martyr the baptismal instructions contained in an enigmatic church order, usually identified as being the *Apostolic Tradition* written by Hippolytus of Rome in the early third century. However, a growing number of scholars believe that this attribution may be mistaken, and so the church order may not reflect Roman practice, nor may its contents necessarily date from the early third century. Instead, it could well be a composite document made up of a number of different elements originating in different time periods, some perhaps as old as the second century, others no older than the early fourth century. In particular, the baptismal instructions seem to reflect at least three different layers of material.[3] Because of this uncertainty about its origin and nature, we shall not use it here to try to establish what baptismal customs might have been at Rome in the century after Justin Martyr. But since one layer of its baptismal material is similar to what we learn from our principal North African witness from this period, Tertullian, we shall note those parallels as we examine his testimony.

North Africa

Tertullian, writing around the beginning of the third century, does not offer a single continuous account of the baptismal ritual, but from the various references to it that are scattered throughout his writings, we can reconstruct the process known to him.[4]

The preferred baptismal season

The Passover [Easter] provides the day of most solemnity for baptism, for then was accomplished our Lord's passion, and into it we are

---

[3] See further Paul F. Bradshaw, Maxwell E. Johnson and L. Edward Phillips, *The Apostolic Tradition: A Commentary* (Fortress Press, Minneapolis 2002).

[4] Nearly all texts cited are taken from *DBL*, pp. 9–11.

baptized . . . After that, Pentecost is a most auspicious period for arrang-
ing baptisms, for during it our Lord's resurrection was several times
made known among the disciples, and the grace of the Holy Spirit first
given . . . For all that, every day is a Lord's day: any hour, any season
is suitable for baptism.   (*De baptismo* 19)

This was apparently not just an idiosyncratic idea of Tertullian's,
for we find the same preference for Easter expressed in Hippolytus'
Commentary on Daniel 1.16, traditionally assumed to come from
Rome. This suggests that in these places there were the beginnings
of a recovery of Paul's theology of baptism as participation in the
death and resurrection of Christ.

Preparation

Those who are at the point of entering upon baptism ought to pray,
with frequent prayers, fastings, bendings of the knee, and all-night
vigils, along with the confession of all their sins, so as to make a copy
of the baptism of John.   (*De baptismo* 20)

Like the Syrian sources, Tertullian does not indicate whether there
was a formally structured catechumenate lasting for an extended
length of time, but there was no doubt some period of instruction,
and this quotation implies the existence of a final stage of preparation
that was particularly expressive of repentance.

Apostolic Tradition 15–20, on the other hand, contains much more
extensive directions for the period of preparation, including the expect-
ation that the catechumenate will normally last three years, a list of
occupations deemed incompatible with being a Christian (most of
which can be paralleled in Tertullian's works), as well as the careful
examination of witnesses as to the candidates' conduct during their
catechumenate in order to ensure that a real change in their way of
life had taken place before they were admitted to hear 'the gospel' in
the final stage of their preparation for baptism. This examination
seems to be parallel to the profession of faith in the Syrian *Didascalia*,
and also leaves its mark in much later Roman texts, where what is
known as the Scrutiny has become an exorcism of the candidates.
Vestiges of older practices in a number of later sources from various
parts of the world suggest that at one time this final stage lasted
for three weeks, which may well have been the custom known to
Tertullian.

Prayer over the water

> All waters, when God is invoked, acquire the sacred significance of conveying sanctity: for at once the Spirit comes down from heaven and stays upon the waters, sanctifying them from within himself, and when thus sanctified they absorb the power of sanctifying... Thus when the waters have in some sense acquired healing power by an angel's intervention, the spirit is in those waters corporally washed, while the flesh is in those same waters spiritually cleansed.
>
> (*De baptismo* 4)

Tertullian is the very first person to mention the invocation of the Holy Spirit over the water, and it probably arose as a result of the change in the location of baptisms, from rivers and lakes to indoor baths or tanks, to which we earlier saw the *Didache* allude. While the naturally flowing character of the former could enable them to be seen as 'living' and already imbued with God's spirit, the water in the latter would have seemed deficient in this respect, and hence in need of investing with the power that they lacked. We have already seen this happening with regard to the oil used in Syria, and it is interesting to note that Tertullian describes the power bestowed on the sanctified water as that of healing, as is also the case with Syrian oil. He is insistent, however, that though the Holy Spirit is active in the water, it is not the source from which the candidates will receive the Spirit: 'Not that in the waters we obtain the Holy Spirit; but in the water under [the witness of] the angel we are cleansed and prepared for the Holy Spirit' (*De baptismo* 11.1).

The renunciation of evil

> When on the point of coming to the water we then and there, as also somewhat earlier in church under the hand of the bishop, affirm that we renounce the devil and his pomp and his angels.   (*De corona* 3)

Tertullian's description suggests that the renunciation happened more than once during the period of preparation for baptism as well as immediately before the immersion. Elsewhere he speaks of renouncing 'the devil, his retinue, and his works' (*De spectaculis* 4). It may have been in the form of a direct address to the devil by the candidate, such as is attested in the *Apostolic Tradition*, 'I renounce you, Satan, and all your service and all your works'; or it may have been in the form of a response to a question put to the candidate ('Do you

19

renounce . . .'), such as we find in later sources, often divided into three parts (Satan, works, pomps), in order to parallel the threefold profession of faith.[5]

The triple profession of faith and triple immersion

> When we have entered the water, we make profession of the Christian faith in the words of its rule. *(De spectaculis* 4)

> We are three times immersed, while we answer interrogations rather more extensive than our Lord has prescribed in the gospel.
> *(De corona* 3)

> For not once only, but three times are we baptized into each of the three persons at each of the several names. *(Adversus Praxean* 26)

> The flesh is washed that the soul may be made spotless.
> *(De resurrectione carnis* 8)

Tertullian's brief references do not supply a very clear picture of the practice, but we can fill out what is probably in mind by means of the more detailed directions in *Apostolic Tradition* 21. If one peels away what seem to be later additions here, it appears that the original directed:

> As he who is to be baptized is descending into the water, let him who baptizes him say thus: 'Do you believe in God the Father omnipotent?' And let the one being baptized say, 'I believe.' And the giver, having his hand placed on his head, shall baptize him once. And then he shall say: 'Do you believe in Christ Jesus, the Son of God?' And when he has said, 'I believe', he shall be baptized again. And he shall say again: 'Do you believe in the Holy Spirit and the holy Church and the resurrection of the flesh?' Then he who is being baptized shall say, 'I believe', and thus he shall be baptized a third time.

One can easily see that it was out of baptismal professions of faith of this kind that the so-called Apostles' Creed evolved; and it had doubtless been the transition from a simple declaration of faith in Jesus to a trinitarian affirmation that had caused the immersion also to assume a triple character.

---

[5] See *DBL*, p. 230 for the later Roman form. At Milan, at least from the time of Ambrose onwards, the question was in two parts (devil and his works; the world and its pleasures – later, his world and his pomps): *DBL*, pp. 178, 181, 187, 194, 199.

This element constitutes one of the most striking differences from Syrian practice. While in Syria the candidates' expression of belief took place on an earlier occasion, and the immersion was accompanied by a trinitarian formula spoken over the candidate, here the trinitarian profession of faith itself in effect constituted the baptismal formula. It thus offered a vivid visual representation of the intimate connection that was understood to exist between faith and baptism. For there was no suggestion for Tertullian or other early Christian theologians that baptism could somehow 'work' without the presence of faith in the candidate. Tertullian himself affirmed: 'that washing is a sealing of faith, which faith is begun and is commended by the faith of repentance. We are not washed in order that we may cease sinning, but because we have ceased, since in heart we have been bathed already' (*De paenitentia* 6). Similarly, Origen in Alexandria maintained that 'if someone who is still sinning comes to the bath, he does not receive the forgiveness of sins' (*Homiliae in Lucam* 21). Naturally, the requirement of faith presented something of a problem in the case of infant baptism, as we shall see in a later chapter.

Post-baptismal anointing

> After that we come up from the washing and are anointed with the blessed unction, following that ancient practice by which, ever since Aaron was anointed by Moses, there was a custom of anointing them for priesthood with oil out of a horn. That is why [the high priest] is called a Christ, from 'chrism' which is [the Greek for] 'anointing' and from this also our Lord obtained his title, though it had become a spiritual anointing, in that he was anointed with the Spirit of God the Father.
>
> (*De baptismo* 7)

> The flesh is anointed that the soul may be consecrated.
>
> (*De resurrectione carnis* 8)

Here we encounter a close parallel to the anointing and its interpretation found in the Syrian *Didascalia* – but in a quite different position, following rather than preceding the immersion and apparently of the head alone, not the whole body.

Sign of the cross

> The flesh is signed [with the cross] that the soul too may be protected.
>
> (*De resurrectione carnis* 8)

21

Tertullian apparently understands this post-baptismal ceremony to have a protective function, God's mark on a person being able to ward off evil powers.

Imposition of hands with prayer

> Next follows the imposition of the hand in benediction, inviting and welcoming the Holy Spirit. (*De baptismo* 8)

> The flesh is overshadowed by the imposition of the hand that the soul may be illumined by the Spirit. (*De resurrectione carnis* 8)

Here is another major difference from Syrian practice, not merely in the presence of a post-baptismal imposition of hands, but in Tertullian's linking of that particular gesture with the gift of the Holy Spirit. Cyprian, Bishop of Carthage in North Africa in the middle of the third century, confirms the continuing existence of this same tradition: the newly baptized are brought to the bishops 'and by our prayers and by the imposition of hands obtain the Holy Spirit, and are perfected with the Lord's seal' (*Epistulae* 73.9). He associates this with the action in Acts 8 where Peter and John give the Holy Spirit to those who have been baptized by others. There is a similar imposition of hands with prayer in *Apostolic Tradition* 21, and some versions of the text of that prayer connect the action with the bestowal of the Spirit, while others speak of the baptized having already received the Spirit through their immersion in the water.

Eucharist, including milk and honey

> Made welcome then [into the assembly] we partake of a compound of milk and honey. (*De corona* 3)

> The flesh feeds on the Body and Blood of Christ so that the soul as well may be filled with God. (*De resurrectione carnis* 8)

The same custom, of offering the newly baptized milk and honey together with the bread and wine in the celebration of the Eucharist that concluded their initiation rite, is also attested in *Apostolic Tradition* 21, which explicitly relates its symbolism to the fulfilment of the Old Testament promise that God's people would inherit a land flowing with milk and honey.

4

The fourth-century synthesis

The cessation of persecution in the early fourth century brought a major change in the practice of Christian initiation. Because it was now safe and respectable to become a Christian, there was a considerable increase in the number of people wanting to join the Church. However, not all of these took the step because they had experienced an inner conversion: some did so from less worthy motives, such as the desire to marry a Christian or to please a master or friend, or because it promised to be advantageous to their career or political ambitions. Moreover, once having become catechumens, many people were in no hurry to complete the process of initiation. Since they were already regarded as Christians, they saw no need to proceed to baptism itself, especially as that would leave no second chance to obtain the forgiveness of sins that baptism was believed to convey: it seemed preferable to delay the actual baptism as long as possible so as to be sure of having all one's sins forgiven and so of gaining salvation. Consequently, many parents enrolled their children as catechumens early in their life but delayed presenting them for baptism at least until after the passions of youth had subsided and there was less chance of them succumbing to temptation; and many adults deferred their own baptism until they became seriously ill when they feared they might die unbaptized.

All of this had a profound effect on the nature of the baptismal process itself. Whereas in primitive Christianity it had functioned as a ritual expression of a genuine conversion experience that candidates were already undergoing in their lives, now in the fourth century the baptismal process became instead the means of conveying a profound experience to the candidates in the hope of bringing about their conversion. In order to accomplish this new role, the process became much more dramatic – one might even say theatrical – in character. Taking their cue from contemporary pagan mystery religions, the ceremonies surrounding baptism became highly elaborate and cloaked in such great secrecy that candidates would have no idea in advance what was going to happen to them, with the aim of producing a powerful emotional and psychological impression upon them. Often only after they had experienced the celebration of baptism and the Eucharist was an explanation of the meaning of the sacred mysteries in which they had partaken then given to them in what was called mystagogy – post-baptismal instruction, usually during the week following their initiation.

The frequent lack of obvious signs of conversion in the behaviour of the newly baptized also had a significant impact on baptismal theology in another way. On the one hand, fourth-century preachers continued to insist on the need for real faith and amendment of life if baptism was to be efficacious, just as their predecessors in the third century had done, and engaged in substantial pre-baptismal instruction in order to impress upon the candidates the great importance of the step that they were taking. On the other hand, there was at the same time a growing tendency in theological discussion to focus on the invisible transformation that was believed to take place in baptism rather than to look for visible changes in the conduct of the newly baptized. For example, theologians increasingly understood the term 'seal' from the New Testament not as a vivid metaphor but as a metaphysical reality: as the invisible imprint of the divine image upon the human soul.

Another major characteristic of Christian initiation in the fourth century was a tendency for the varied baptismal practices in the different regions of early Christianity to coalesce into a more homogeneous pattern. The primary sources of our information about this are the baptismal homilies delivered by four leading bishops of the period: in the West, Ambrose of Milan; in the East, John Chrysostom (at Antioch), Cyril of Jerusalem, and Theodore of Mopsuestia.[1] Table 1 gives a schematic view of their evidence. Not surprisingly, Jerusalem (to which pilgrims were now flocking from both East and West) appears to have been the first Eastern centre of Christianity to incorporate into its liturgical practices certain elements that were similar to Western customs.

---

[1] English translations in *AIR*. There is some doubt as to whether Cyril or his successor John was responsible for the *Mystagogical Catecheses*, but Cyril's authorship will be assumed here.

Table 1 Baptismal practices in the fourth century

Ambrose	Cyril	Chrysostom/Theodore
	Renunciation	Renunciation
	Act of adherence	Act of adherence
'Opening'		Anointing of head
Entry to baptistery	Entry to baptistery	(Chrysostom: 'at night')
(Removal of clothes)	Removal of clothes	Removal of clothes
Anointing of body	Anointing of body	Anointing of body
Renunciation		
Blessing of water	(Blessing of water)	Blessing of water
Immersion with profession of faith	Immersion with profession of faith	Immersion with trinitarian formula
Anointing of head	Anointing of head, ears, nose, chest	
Washing of feet		
(White garment)	White garment	White garment
'Sealing'		(Theodore: seal on forehead)
		(Chrysostom: kiss)
Eucharist	Eucharist	Eucharist

The baptismal season

The choice of a preferred season for baptisms serves as a good example of this development. As we have seen, in Egypt the conclusion of the 40-day post-Epiphany fast seems to have become the normal occasion for the celebration of baptism; Rome and North Africa had a preference for Easter; and the Syrian tradition does not appear to have known of any preferential time. By the middle of the fourth century, however, we find an almost universal custom of Easter as the preferred season for all baptisms with the 40-day season of Lent prefixed to it and serving as an extended period of preparation for the baptismal candidates in place of the three-week period of final preparation previously established in many places.

Along with this development – not surprisingly – went the gradual adoption of the Pauline theology of baptism as participation in the death and resurrection of Christ. Thus Cyril, while retaining elements of the older baptismal imagery of the Syrian tradition as birth to new life, adds to it the understanding of the whole process as a symbolic imitation of the passion of Christ. He says to the newly baptized:

> Stripped naked, in this too you were imitating Christ naked on the cross . . . Then you were conducted by the hand to the holy pool of sacred baptism, just as Christ was conveyed from the cross to the sepulchre . . . and submerged yourselves three times in the water and emerged: by this symbolic gesture you were secretly re-enacting the burial of Christ three days in the tomb.[2]

Thus the baptismal font was now portrayed as both womb and tomb.

The catechumenate

The Lenten season included both the preliminary ethical instruction of catechumens, based on the Old Testament, and the creedal/doctrinal teaching formerly reserved for the final three weeks, with the rituals that had originally marked the transition between the two stages now mostly being moved towards the end, immediately before the baptismal rite itself. Those who wished to be baptized at Easter had their names recorded at the beginning of Lent (after being admitted as catechumens, if this had not previously happened); and during this time of preparation there occurred not only the instruction and fasting of which earlier sources had spoken, but also the exorcism of the candidates, the frequency of which varied from place to place: while at Carthage in North Africa it seems to have happened only once, at Rome it occurred on three successive Sundays, and at Antioch and Jerusalem it was repeated daily.[3]

Apart from *Apostolic Tradition* 18 (where it is prescribed on a daily basis), this regular exorcism of all baptismal candidates is clearly attested for the first time only in fourth-century sources, but it is probably an older custom, and has its roots in the New Testament practice of driving out evil spirits from those thought to be possessed. At some unknown point in the history of the Church, this action was extended from particular individuals to every convert, reflecting the early Christian belief that all pagans were in the possession of the

---

[2] *Mystagogical Catechesis* 2.2–4 (*AIR*, pp. 76–8).
[3] *DBL*, pp. 28, 34, 44, 151, 205, 209, 213–15.

devil and needed to be liberated in order to become Christians and receive the Holy Spirit. The same attitude is reflected in the prohibition in *Apostolic Tradition* 18 against catechumens either praying with or exchanging a ritual kiss with baptized Christians, because they were still impure.

Both *Apostolic Tradition* 18 and Ambrose describe a final preparatory ceremony in which the bishop touches the ears and noses of the candidates (and the forehead, too, in the *Apostolic Tradition*). In the *Apostolic Tradition* this action follows an exorcism, involves the sign of the cross and is clearly intended as a 'sealing', to protect the candidates against the return of evil spirits. Ambrose, however, describes it as an 'opening', and interprets it in the light of Jesus' opening of the ears and mouth of a man who was deaf and dumb (Mark 7.32–37), but he has some difficulty in explaining why it is the nose and not the mouth that is touched by the bishop, and he has to resort to saying that it is so that candidates may be 'the aroma of Christ to God' (2 Corinthians 2.15).[4] There are signs both in Ambrose's writings and also in other later Roman sources that this 'opening' had previously functioned as the gateway to the three-week period of final pre-baptismal instruction, before it was expanded into Lent.

The pre-baptismal anointing

As we can see from Table 1, both Eastern and Western rites now have a pre-baptismal anointing. We do not know when the practice was introduced in the West. Although it appears in the *Apostolic Tradition*, we cannot be sure how ancient this part of the text is. Its role there is described as exorcistic and it is applied with the words, 'Let every evil spirit depart from you'. Ambrose, however, describes the practice in slightly different terms: he speaks of the candidates being 'rubbed with oil like an athlete, Christ's athlete, as though in preparation for an earthly wrestling-match'.[5] In spite of these differences, both sources agree that it functioned in some way against the power of evil, whether as a protective shield or as preparatory for combat with the devil. It is to be noted that what is being described in both cases

---

[4] *De sacramentis* 1.2–3 (*AIR*, pp. 100–1).
[5] *De sacramentis* 1.4 (*AIR*, p. 102).

is an anointing of the whole body – just as we found in some of the third-century Syrian examples. It looks, therefore, as though this development may possibly have spread from East to West, or alternatively both regions may have been influenced by similar uses of oil in contemporary pagan traditions.

On the other hand, when we turn to the Syrian sources, we find that both Chrysostom and Theodore distinguish an anointing of the forehead from the anointing of the whole body that follows it (and according to Chrysostom, perfumed oil – chrism – is used for the purpose). Theodore states that the first of these is accompanied by the recitation of the trinitarian formula and constitutes a 'seal' that 'marks you out for ever as the sheep of Christ, the soldier of the King of Heaven': just as a sheep is branded to indicate its owner and a soldier is given a tattoo to indicate the Emperor to whom he owes his allegiance, so too the Christian can be identified as 'a soldier of the true king and a citizen of heaven'.[6] Chrysostom, too, compares this anointing to the branding of a sheep,[7] and also uses the images of both soldier and athlete at this point, but he focuses more on its protective character, which will 'make the devil turn away his eyes'.[8]

Theodore tells us that the same trinitarian formula is used for the anointing of the whole body, but he views this ceremony as symbolic of clothing, 'a sign of the garment of immortality you will receive through baptism'.[9] Chrysostom, on the other hand, describes it in protective terms again, like the previous anointing, intended to 'armour all your limbs and make them invulnerable to any weapons the Enemy may hurl'.[10] Cyril speaks of only one anointing before baptism, that of the whole body, and interprets it both as exorcistic in nature, 'able to pursue all the invisible powers of the wicked one out of our persons', and also as a symbol of the share that the candidate will have in the richness of Christ the true olive tree.[11]

---

[6] *Baptismal Homily* 2.17–19 (*AIR*, pp. 177–9).

[7] See Paul W. Harkins, *St John Chrysostom: Baptismal Instructions* (Longmans, Green, & Co., London 1963), p. 155.

[8] *Baptismal Homily* 2.22–3 (*AIR*, p. 160).

[9] *Baptismal Homily* 3.8 (*AIR*, p. 185).

[10] *Baptismal Homily* 2.24 (*AIR*, p. 161).

[11] *Mystagogical Catechesis* 2.3 (*AIR*, p. 77).

While these explanations of pre-baptismal anointing differ to some extent from one another, what they have in common is that none of them views the anointing of the head in the same way as some of the earlier Syrian sources had done and as East Syrian sources of the period continued to do – as a priestly anointing or as the conferral of the Holy Spirit.

The profession of faith and immersion

The Eastern and Western traditions retain some of their former characteristics here. The acts of renunciation and adherence to Christ remain at the beginning of the Eastern rites, while Ambrose attests that in his region the triple immersion in water was still accompanied by a threefold profession of faith in interrogatory form, similar to that evidenced earlier by Tertullian and the *Apostolic Tradition*.[12] (We should note, however, that some Christian groups that rejected trinitarian orthodoxy reverted to just a single immersion at baptism in order to give liturgical expression to their doctrinal position, and some orthodox Christians revised the Eastern act of adherence so that it was made to the Trinity, in order to reflect their position.) On the other hand, in Jerusalem a Western-style interrogatory form of profession of faith has been added at the time of the immersion;[13] and the Syrian baptismal formula ('I baptize you in the name . . .') had already begun to be adopted in Egypt, and would gradually spread westwards during the fifth and sixth centuries. Its introduction there would separate the profession of faith from its original close connection with the immersion and force it into a preliminary position just before it. Because of this change in the rite, it would be easier for later theologians to disregard the vital part that the candidate's own faith had once played in the process of becoming a Christian and to emphasize instead the action of divine grace.

Meanwhile, in Syria itself, Chrysostom reveals that the baptismal formula there had undergone a significant change in wording. Because the active form ('I baptize . . .') had seemed to lay too great an emphasis on the role of the minister, a passive form ('N. is baptized . . .') was

---

[12] *De sacramentis* 2.20 (*AIR*, p. 118).
[13] *Mystagogical Catechesis* 2.4 (*AIR*, pp. 77–8).

now being used instead, and this later became standard in all Eastern rites. Chrysostom also claims that 'by the words of the bishop and by his hand the presence of the Holy Spirit flies down upon you'. The 'words' were the baptismal formula, and the hand was placed on the candidate's head in order to push him or her down under the water. Thus Chrysostom appears to envisage the Holy Spirit being bestowed in the act of immersion itself, as the *Didascalia* had previously done, and not through any ancillary ceremonies, although in line with the new orthodoxy of the period he is also careful to insist that it is 'the indivisible Trinity who bring the whole rite to completion'.[14]

Post-baptismal ceremonies

Ambrose refers to an unction of the head with chrism after baptism, during which the bishop simply speaks of God anointing the newly baptized 'into eternal life'. The brevity of his comments on this ceremony suggests that Ambrose himself did not attach much importance to it. He interprets it as a pouring of grace upon the faculties of wisdom in the head, but elsewhere he does allude to the royal and priestly symbolism that Tertullian had earlier emphasized.[15] Ambrose devotes more time instead to defending the appropriateness of the ceremony of the washing of the feet of the newly baptized that immediately follows. He interprets it as providing protection against the liability to sin inherited from Adam.[16] Although none of our other principal sources include it in their rites, there are signs that it was also practised in a number of other places, and it may even at one time have sufficed instead of full immersion in some communities. Finally, Ambrose refers to a 'spiritual sealing' concluding the rite, during which the Holy Spirit was infused at the invocation of the bishop,[17] but he is not explicit as to what this 'sealing' was. It seems most likely to have been an imposition of hands with prayer (as in Tertullian) or a simple concluding prayer (as in the later Milanese rites), but a second post-baptismal anointing (as in *Apostolic Tradition*

---

[14] *Baptismal Homily* 2.25–6 (*AIR*, pp. 161–2).

[15] *De sacramentis* 2.24; 3.1; 4.3 (*AIR*, pp. 119–20, 128).

[16] *De sacramentis* 3.4–7 (*AIR*, pp. 121–3).

[17] *De sacramentis* 3.8–10 (*AIR*, pp. 124–5).

21 and later Roman evidence) or the sign of the cross, or even a kiss, have also been suggested.

Although Chrysostom's rite continued the older Syrian tradition of passing directly from the immersion to the exchange of a kiss and then to the celebration of the Eucharist and reception of communion by the newly baptized, Theodore's description includes a reference to a 'sealing' on the forehead at the end of the rite. This apparently involved the use of oil and was accompanied by a trinitarian formula. Theodore understands it as a sign that the Holy Spirit had been bestowed upon the baptized.[18] While some scholars have rejected this passage as a later interpolation into the text, others see it as evidence for the emergence of a post-baptismal unction associated with the gift of the Spirit in the Syrian tradition.

At Jerusalem, something similar to the Western post-baptismal anointing has certainly emerged by this time. However, what Cyril describes is not just an anointing of the head, as in Tertullian and Ambrose, but one that also encompassed ears, nose and chest. Although acknowledging that this anointing (which was done with chrism) was foreshadowed in priestly and kingly anointings in the Old Testament, Cyril likens it to the anointing with the Spirit that Christ received after his baptism. He explains that the anointing of the forehead is done so that the newly baptized may lose the shame of Adam, the ears so that they may hear divine mysteries, the nose so that they may become 'the aroma of Christ to God', and the chest to arm them against the devil.[19] The presence of these images suggests that the association of the Holy Spirit with this action was a more recent addition to an anointing that had previously had a rather different purpose.

All three Eastern bishops – Chrysostom, Cyril and Theodore – say that the newly baptized do not simply put on their own clothes again but dress in special white garments, as a symbol of the purity of their new life (Cyril), of Christ whom they have put on internally (Chrysostom), of their future resurrection (Theodore). Ambrose alludes only indirectly to this practice, which reminds him of the shining garments of the transfigured Christ.[20]

---

[18] *Baptismal Homily* 3.27 (*AIR*, pp. 198–9).

[19] *Mystagogical Catechesis* 3 (*AIR*, pp. 81–5).

[20] *AIR*, pp. 31–3, 88–9, 129, 144, 197–8.

Thus, there are certainly still significant differences in the structure of the rites between East and West (and within each of those regions, too), and different emphases in their interpretation, and especially in relation to where they locate the giving of the Spirit: in the pre-baptismal anointing of the head (East Syria), in the baptismal water itself (Chrysostom in West Syria), in a post-baptismal anointing (Jerusalem), or in a further post-baptismal 'sealing', probably prayer and/or laying on of hands (Ambrose). Nevertheless, by the close of the fourth century a more homogeneous initiation rite is beginning to emerge, and a rich mixture of images and symbols drawn from both the New Testament and other sources is being used to explain its meaning.

5

From adult to infant baptism

It is not at all certain when baptism began to be extended to infants as well as older children and adults. The first undisputed reference to the custom occurs in North Africa at the beginning of the third century in the writings of Tertullian, who disapproves of it.[1] However, some scholars have argued that infant baptism was not an innovation at this period but a traditional practice going back to the first century. Much depends upon how references to baptisms of a 'household' in the New Testament (Acts 16.15; 1 Corinthians 1.16) should be understood: did that term include very young children or not? On the other hand, even if the practice of infant baptism had been adopted at an early date, it did not quickly replace adult baptism as the norm everywhere. While Cyprian in North Africa in the third century insisted that there was no need to wait until the eighth day after birth to baptize an infant, as some were claiming on the basis of the biblical prescription for circumcision (*Epistulae* 64), Gregory of Nazianzus in Cappadocia in 381 advised that children should normally be baptized at about the age of three years, when they were able to answer the baptismal questions themselves and could to some extent understand the Christian faith (*Orationes* 40.28)! There are also plenty of examples of people from Christian families in the fourth century who were not baptized until they had become adults, including Augustine himself. Indeed, as we saw in the previous chapter, there was a widespread tendency at that time to delay baptism as long as possible. Thus, Anthony Lane's argument that there was a pluriform practice in early Christianity, some churches baptizing infants from earliest times onwards and others normally not, seems the most likely answer to the question.[2]

---

[1] *De baptismo* 18 (*DBL*, p. 10).

[2] Anthony N. S. Lane, 'Did the Apostolic Church Baptise Babies? A Seismological Approach', *Tyndale Bulletin* 55 (2004), pp. 109–30.

The profession of faith

We have seen in earlier chapters that a profession of faith by the candidates themselves was a central element in the baptismal process. When, therefore, infants were to be baptized, this obviously created something of a difficulty. The problem was resolved by allowing someone else to speak on their behalf. Thus *Apostolic Tradition* 21 directs that 'as for those who cannot speak for themselves, their parents or someone from their family shall speak for them'. Fifth-century sources indicate that a similar action was also taken in the case of adult candidates who had signified their desire for baptism but were too ill to answer for themselves when the time came, and this may even have constituted the precedent for doing this for infants.

However, none of the earliest sources offers any theological justification for presuming that the infants themselves possessed faith that could be professed on their behalf. The closest that Cyprian came to it was to say that infants' crying constituted their petition to be baptized (*Epistulae* 64.6). Thus it looks as though practice may have preceded doctrine here, perhaps simply as a result of an inchoate desire on the part of Christian parents to have their children share in whatever benefits they believed themselves to enjoy as a result of baptism. It was only later in the writings of Augustine of Hippo (354–430) that a theological explanation for infant baptism first appeared that was eventually to become the standard explanation in traditional Catholic theology. This was that belief was not a prerequisite for baptism as it was in the case of an adult, but faith was bestowed on the child through the faith of others in the celebration of the rite itself:

> When, on behalf of an infant as yet incapable of exercising faith, the answer is given that he believes, this answer means that he has faith because of the sacrament of faith . . . Therefore an infant, although he is not yet a believer in the sense of having that faith which includes the consenting will of those who exercise it, nevertheless becomes a believer through the sacrament of that faith. For as it is answered that he believes, so also he is called a believer, not because he assents to the truth by an act of his own judgment, but because he receives the sacrament of that truth.[3]

---

[3] *Epistulae* 98.9, 10. English translation from Philip Schaff (ed.), *A Select Library of the Nicene and Post-Nicene Fathers of the Christian Church* (T&T Clark, Edinburgh 1886–1900), vol. 1, p. 410.

As this quotation implies, and as is confirmed from elsewhere in Augustine's writings, a change was made in the wording of the profession of faith in his church when infants were being baptized. Whereas, when the candidate was an adult or older child, this profession was in the form of a series of direct questions and answers ('Do you believe . . . ?' 'I believe'[4]), at the baptism of an infant both the questions and the responses made on behalf of the candidate were instead cast in the third person: 'Does he/she believe . . . ?' 'He/she believes.'[5] This variation was enough to cause Augustine's theological opponent Pelagius to argue that, if adults and infants were supposed to be receiving the same baptism, then exactly the same words ought to be used in the rite.[6]

Although there are signs that this form of the profession of faith was also adopted in the case of infants in Spain and France as well as Northern Africa, it did not apparently affect the practice at Rome, which was always particularly conservative in liturgical matters. Consequently, when the Roman rite eventually supplanted all other local rites in the West during the Middle Ages, the use of the adult formula for infants became universal. This effectively reduced the role of the godparent in the rite to that of a mere ventriloquist, supplying a voice for the silent child.

The trend towards infant baptism as the norm

By the fifth century the same beliefs that at first had caused people to delay baptism began to lead them in the opposite direction: if baptism was necessary for salvation, was it not desirable to baptize children as young as possible, lest they should happen to die and forfeit their opportunity for salvation? This tendency was given strong impetus both by the high infant mortality rate in the ancient world and in the West by the theological reflections of Augustine, who argued that because the Church practised the baptism of infants, it must follow that babies were thus in need of the remission of sin that baptism brought. Since newborn children had not yet committed actual sins, he concluded that they must have inherited

---

[4] See above, p. 20.
[5] See Augustine, *Epistulae* 98.7; *Sermones* 294.12.
[6] See Augustine, *De gratia Christi et de peccato originali* 1.32.35; 2.1.1; 2.21.24.

the 'original sin' of Adam: 'What need is there, therefore, for an infant to be conformed to the death of Christ through baptism, if he is not completely poisoned by the serpent's bite?'[7] Augustine was not the first to reason in this way from practice to doctrine. Both Cyprian and Origen in the third century had drawn similar conclusions from infant baptism,[8] in contrast to earlier Christian theologians who had asserted the purity of newborn children. Augustine not only developed the idea more fully, but he added a powerful motivation for conferring baptism at the earliest possible age, since he argued that children dying unbaptized would inevitably be damned, although he believed that they would receive only 'the mildest condemnation'.[9]

It was not long, therefore, before infant baptism became more or less universal throughout the Christian Church, and people forgot that baptism had originally been connected with adult conversions. Indeed, some Western texts from the tenth century onwards offer an amusing illustration of the extent to which infant baptisms came to be considered as normative. They direct that infants are to be held in the right arms of their sponsor, and adult candidates are to place their foot upon the foot of their sponsor – the latter apparently an attempt to conform as closely as possible to what was done in the case of infants! It is also an indication of the extent to which the role of sponsor or godparent had changed: from being the person who presented an adult candidate for baptism and vouched for the genuineness of the conversion that had already taken place in his or her life, the godparent was now the one who held the baby at the ceremony and made the responses to the questions concerning faith on his or her behalf, and in later medieval rites was also charged with the future spiritual upbringing of the child.[10]

---

[7] *De peccatorum meritis et remissione* 1.61.

[8] Cyprian, *Epistulae* 64.5; Origen, *Homiliae in Leviticum* 8; *Homiliae in Lucam* 14; *Commentarii in epistulam ad Romanos* 5.9.

[9] *De peccatorum meritis et remissione* 1.21.

[10] For a detailed study of the role of the godparent, see Joseph H. Lynch, *Godparents and Kinship in Early Medieval Europe* (Princeton University Press, Princeton 1986).

The emergence of 'confirmation'

At first, infants tended to be treated in the same way as adult candidates, including their participation in the ritual elements of the catechumenate. Thus in the church at Rome, for example, they would be brought to church at the beginning of Lent and enrolled in the catechumenate; they would be presented on subsequent Sundays during the Lenten season to receive exorcism and to have the Creed, the Lord's Prayer, and the opening verses of the four Gospels read to them, even though they were incapable of comprehending what was said; and they would receive the full rite of initiation at Easter.[11]

However, given the high infant mortality rate of the times, many infants were not healthy enough to wait until Easter each year to be baptized, and so in those cases a similar procedure was adopted as for adults who were in imminent danger of death: the demands and rituals of the catechumenate were simply eliminated from the process and the baptism was performed without delay, frequently being delegated to a local presbyter rather than waiting until the candidate could be taken to the bishop (who would normally have presided over it). It is important to note, however, that for both adults and infants it was the full initiation rite that was usually performed: all the pre- and post-baptismal ceremonies, such as anointing or the imposition of hands, were generally included, and the newly baptized received Holy Communion either at their baptism or soon afterwards. The only modification that might be made was that if the candidates were very ill or weak, rather than being immersed in the water, water could be poured over them instead.

But here Rome constituted an exception. Because of the large number of Christian congregations in the city, presbyters had apparently been accustomed from early times to perform the initiation rites themselves, but it was expected that the newly baptized would be taken to the bishop as soon as possible afterwards for the final element of the process, the 'sealing' (by which an imposition of hands seems to be meant), if the bishop were not himself present at the baptism to do it. We saw that tradition reflected earlier in relation to the baptism of Novatian, and also a similar emphasis given by Cyprian

---

[11] See *DBL*, pp. 212–25.

in North Africa to a post-baptismal 'sealing' performed by the bishop with prayer and the imposition of hands (see above, pp. 16, 22).

By the end of the fourth century this 'sealing' at Rome was accompanied by a second post-baptismal anointing – no doubt in order to make the ceremony more dramatic – as this letter written in 416 from Pope Innocent I to Decentius, Bishop of Gubbio, shows:

> Concerning the sealing of the newly-baptized, it is clear that this may not be done by anyone other than the bishop. For even though presbyters are priests, they do not hold the office of pontiff. Not only does ecclesiastical custom show that this ought to be done by pontiffs alone – that they seal and deliver the Spirit, the Paraclete – but so does that reading in the Acts of the Apostles which tells how Peter and John were directed to deliver the Holy Spirit to those who had already been baptized. For when presbyters baptize, either without the bishop or in the bishop's presence, they are allowed to anoint the baptized with chrism, as long as it has been consecrated by the bishop, but not to sign the forehead with the same oil, which is reserved to bishops alone when they deliver the Spirit, the Paraclete.[12]

The desire to retain the bishop's personal involvement in some part of the initiation process rather than delegate the whole rite to presbyters in the case of emergency baptisms, as churches in other parts of the world were doing, is perfectly understandable and did not really mean the destruction of the unity of the baptismal rite, because the delay between the two parts would usually have been very short. It was only when the practice was extended in later centuries to other parts of the Western Church, as a result of the expansion of Roman influence, that it ceased to work nearly as well. For in northern Europe, dioceses were very large in size and travel often much more difficult, particularly in winter. As a result, the delay between baptism and what was now called 'confirmation' grew much longer, until the two came to be thought of as quite separate sacraments belonging to different points in a person's life.[13]

---

[12] Latin text in Robert Cabié (ed.), *La Lettre du pape Innocent 1er à Décentius de Gubbio* (Publications Universitaires de Louvain, Louvain 1973), pp. 22–4.

[13] For more details of this development, see J. D. C. Fisher, *Christian Initiation: Baptism in the Medieval West* (SPCK, London 1965), pp. 120–40.

Part 2

EUCHARIST

In this section we shall not follow the development of rites and their theology in precisely the same chronological manner as we did in the case of Christian initiation, where we looked at different regional traditions and traced their gradual coming together. Instead we shall examine several strands of thought and practice that apparently existed alongside one another in nearly every early Christian tradition, and observe how those strands intertwined in the course of the first few centuries.

Suggestions for further reading

In addition to works cited in notes, the following are recommended:

Paul F. Bradshaw, *Eucharistic Origins* (SPCK, London 2004).

Paul F. Bradshaw, *Reconstructing Early Christian Worship* (SPCK, London 2009), chapters 1–3.

Andrew B. McGowan, *Ascetic Eucharists* (Clarendon Press, Oxford 1999).

6

Sacred meal

The Last Supper

The historical origin of the Christian Eucharist has traditionally been traced back to the Last Supper that Jesus is said to have eaten with his disciples on the night before he died (see Matthew 27.17–30; Mark 14.12–26; Luke 22.7–38; 1 Corinthians 11.23–26). However, we should note that many of the earliest references to the Christian practice outside the New Testament do not link his sayings about the bread and cup being his body and blood specifically with that occasion, and indeed the Fourth Gospel locates Jesus' sayings about bread being his flesh in connection with one of his miraculous feedings (John 6). Scholars increasingly recognize, therefore, that for a proper understanding of the roots of Christian eucharistic practice, the Last Supper needs to be set within the broader context of shared meals that seem to have been characteristic of Jesus and of his first followers.

Sharing a meal together has always been one of the main ways in which human beings have expressed friendship and mutual acceptance, and in the ancient world social life centred around eating and drinking every bit as much as it does for most people today, whether that was a dinner party given at a rich person's house, a regular gathering of the associations that were often formed around a trade guild or profession, or a meeting of one of the 'mystery cults'. Consequently, there has been a good deal of interest among scholars in recent years in the ways in which the earliest Christian assemblies would have resembled such groups.

There has also been considerable scholarly debate about whether or not the Last Supper was a Passover meal. While the three synoptic Gospels state that it was, the Gospel of John places it on the day before the Passover, with Jesus' death occurring on the day of the Passover. However, for our purposes, this question is not particularly crucial. For, even if the Last Supper *were* a Passover meal, no practices that were exclusive to that festive meal seem to have been retained in the primitive Church's eucharistic celebrations; and even if it *were not* a Passover meal, it still took place within a Passover atmosphere and context, and so it is not surprising to find images and ideas from that festival turning up in later Christian eucharistic theology.

Religious meals in Judaism

One of the forms of sacrifice in the Temple was what is known as a 'communion-sacrifice', in which those who had brought the sacrifice consumed part of it together, thus uniting themselves to one another and to God in a ritual meal (see below, p. 62). However, sacred meals in Judaism were not limited merely to practices connected with the Temple cult. Among the more pious, and especially the Pharisees, every meal came to be thought of as a religious occasion, and included the blessing of God for the gift of the various things to be eaten or drunk. Such people were, moreover, very careful about not only *what* they ate (so as to observe the dietary laws prescribed in the Old Testament) but also *with whom* they shared a meal, since eating with those they regarded as impure would compromise their own ritual purity. It was for this reason that Jesus' behaviour scandalized many of his contemporaries, since, although apparently claiming to be a pious Jew, he ate with the outcasts of society – tax-collectors and sinners (see, for example, Matthew 9.10–13; Mark 2.15–17; Luke 5.29–32).

Furthermore, it was a regular part of Jewish eschatological imagery to portray the kingdom of God at the end of time in terms of a great banquet, at which all those who enjoyed God's favour would sit down together and feast in abundance. Jesus continued this tradition in his own teaching (see, for example, Matthew 8.11–12; Luke 13.28–29), and it forms one of the strands in the accounts of the Last Supper: the three synoptic Gospels all record in one form or another a saying of Jesus to the effect that 'I shall not drink again of the fruit of the vine until that day when I drink it new in the kingdom of God' (Mark 14.25; see also Matthew 26.29; Luke 22.15, 18). Similarly, his feeding miracles and the other meals that he shared must also be viewed in this light, as symbolic anticipations of the future messianic banquet, so that those who eat with him now are assured that they will also feast with him in the age to come.

Thus, all the meals Jesus shared with his followers, and not merely the Last Supper, were seen by the early Christians as expressing not only human companionship but also the participants' communion with one another and with God. Hence their presence at their own ritual meals was a sign of their reconciliation to God and membership among the elect who would one day feast together in God's kingdom, and the intimate association with one another that they experienced around the table was a foretaste, an anticipation, of the union that they would enjoy for ever with God. The whole meal event was thus both a prophetic symbol of the future and also a means of entering into that future in the present.

Feeding the hungry

In Graeco-Roman culture, the rich were expected to invite not only their friends but also those who were financially dependent on them to dine with them (even if the latter were not always provided with the same quality of food as those who were socially superior), and the wealthy patron might afterwards send them home with the leftovers or distribute whatever remained from the meal to others who had not been present. Not surprisingly, especially given Jesus' concern for the poor and outcasts in society, the sharing of food with the needy seems to have been a very important aspect of the early Christian movement, and it appears that at Jerusalem if not elsewhere there was a regular distribution of food to widows, who would have been among the most indigent members of the Christian community (Acts 6.1). It also explains why St Paul was so angry about the behaviour of the Christians at Corinth. For, at their eucharistic meals, individuals were apparently failing to share out the food that they had brought, so that the poor remained hungry while others overindulged. What was happening was thus the exact opposite of the intimate unity and the care for one another that the meal was supposed to express, so that Paul concludes that 'it is not the Lord's supper that you eat' (1 Corinthians 11.20). And it explains the adoption in some places of the Greek name *agape* ('love') for the eucharistic meal, since it was one of the principal ways that Christians showed their love for one another.[1]

The intimate connection that was seen between sharing the Christian meal together and caring for those in need continued in later practice. Justin Martyr, writing in the middle of the second century, concludes his description of the weekly Eucharist by stating that

> those who have the means and so desire give what they wish, each according to his own choice; and what is collected is deposited with the president. And he provides for both orphans and widows, and those in need through sickness or through other cause, and those who are in prison, and strangers sojourning, and, in a word, he becomes a protector for all those who are in want.   (*First Apology* 67.1, 6–7)

The *Apostolic Tradition* also gives instructions about suppers being given for the benefit of the poor and about food donations for them to take home (chapters 28, 30).

The ritual pattern

The accounts of the Last Supper reveal a pattern that adheres to the common custom followed at all Jewish formal meals. At the beginning of the meal, the head of the household, acting on behalf of the gathering, took bread into his hands, said a short blessing, broke the bread, and shared it with all present; and at the end of the meal, he again took a cup of wine into his hands, said a longer form of blessing or thanksgiving over it, and shared it with all those around the table. This also resembles the standard pattern of a banquet within Graeco-Roman culture, known as the *symposium*, in which wine was generally consumed after the eating had finished rather than alongside it. It has usually been assumed that the earliest Christian Eucharists would at first have followed this same ritual pattern. However, that does not appear to have been so, at least not in every case.

In the Acts of the Apostles, the author claims that the first Christians in Jerusalem regularly 'breaking bread in their homes . . . partook of food with glad and generous hearts' (Acts 2.46; see also 2.42); that on at least one occasion the disciples assembled on the first day of

---

[1] On the meaning of *agape*, see Andrew B. McGowan, 'Naming the Feast: *Agape* and the Diversity of Early Christian Meals', *Studia Patristica* 30 (1997), pp. 314–18.

the week to break bread (Acts 20.7, 11); and that during a stormy voyage when everyone on board had gone without food for 14 days, Paul set an example to the rest by taking bread 'and giving thanks to God in the presence of all he broke it and began to eat' (Acts 27.35). The same author, towards the end of the Gospel of Luke, spoke of two disciples recognizing the risen Jesus 'in the breaking of the bread', when in their home he took bread, said the blessing, broke it, and gave it to them (Luke 24.30–31, 35). Many scholars have understood the expression 'the breaking of the bread' to be merely a shorthand expression for a meal in which both bread and wine would have been consumed, but that assumption seems unwarranted, especially as the diet of poor people would have consisted almost exclusively of bread and we also know that at least some early Christians down to the third century avoided drinking wine because of its connection with libations to pagan gods and drank water instead at their Eucharists (see Cyprian, *Epistulae* 63), just as others avoided eating meat because it would have been used in pagan sacrifices (see 1 Corinthians 8).

Yet another pattern

In the *Didache*, probably compiled around the time that many of the New Testament books were written, we find a different pattern, one in which wine was used, but where both cup and bread rituals – in that order – preceded the meal (see below, pp. 50–1). Because of this different order, and the absence of any designation of the bread and wine as the body and blood of Christ, some scholars have denied that this was a Eucharist, even though it uses the word 'thanksgiving' (*eucharistia*) to describe the meal. However, a similar order is also found in the instructions for a Christian supper in *Apostolic Tradition* 25–7; in the Jewish sectarian community at Qumran blessings over bread and new wine took place together at the beginning of the meal; later Rabbinic Judaism allowed wine to be blessed before eating; and even at the *symposium* some wine might be taken as an aperitif or consumed during the meal.[2] Thus, it seems likely that early Christian eucharistic meals actually took different forms in different

---

[2] See further Andrew B. McGowan, 'The Inordinate Cup: Issues of Order in Early Eucharistic Drinking', *Studia Patristica* 35 (2001), pp. 283–91.

communities, in some cases involving a sharing of bread alone, or bread and water, in other cases both bread and wine with or without other foods, with the blessing over the cup preceding that over the bread in some traditions or even both being said together in others.

The disappearance of the meal

Many scholars have believed that Eucharist and meal became separated from one another at an early date, and some have even claimed to detect signs of a gradual pulling apart of the two in New Testament texts, but there is no firm evidence for this. For instance, the Eucharist cannot have *preceded* the meal in 1 Corinthians 11, because then the poor arriving late would have missed it altogether. Thus, it seems that the Eucharist as the consumption of a full meal that satisfied physical hunger may have continued rather longer than these scholars have thought, and probably only began to decline somewhere between the middle of the second century and the middle of the third, earlier in some communities, later in others. Nor is it clear why this happened. It may have been as a result of abuses such as those observed by St Paul at Corinth; it may have been because sporadic local bans by the Roman authorities on the meetings of all clubs (which were often centres of political intrigue) prevented Christians from gathering in the evenings; or it may even have been connected with the practical difficulties involved in enabling a large number of people to recline for a meal together in private houses. In addition, it may have been encouraged by a growing emphasis on the significance of the bread and wine in themselves divorced from the context of a communal meal event, an aspect that we will explore in a little more detail in a later chapter. It should also be remembered that because bread constituted the major ingredient of most poor people's meals, the process would more often have involved a reduction from substantial quantity to symbolic token than the elimination of the meal as such.

Even though in the course of time this transition happened everywhere with regard to their formal weekly gatherings, the eucharistic meal did not entirely disappear from Christian experience but lived on in other contexts and especially in frequent assemblies at the graves of the deceased, which formed the central act of piety of most believers and where, like their pagan neighbours, they ate, drank and danced together.

Justin Martyr

Writing in Rome in the middle of the second century, Justin provides what may be the earliest description of a eucharistic celebration which no longer included a full meal, although that is not entirely clear from what he says:

> And on the day called Sunday an assembly is held in one place of all who live in town or country, and the records of the apostles or the writings of the prophets are read for as long as time allows. Then, when the reader has finished, the president in a discourse admonishes and exhorts (us) to imitate these good things. Then we all stand up together and send up prayers; and as we said before, when we have finished praying, bread and wine and water are brought up, and the president likewise sends up prayers and thanksgivings to the best of his ability, and the people assent, saying the Amen; and the (elements over which) thanks have been given are distributed, and everyone partakes; and they are sent through the deacons to those who are not present.[3]

As can be seen, the eucharistic action proper here is now preceded by a service of reading, preaching and intercessory prayer. Scholars have usually understood this to have been a Christian version of Jewish synagogue practice, which included similar elements. They believe that at least those Christians who came from a Jewish background would have originally assembled for this purpose on the Sabbath quite separately from the evening eucharistic meal. But when the meal was eventually abandoned, there would have seemed less point in assembling twice, particularly as the ritual surrounding the bread and wine was so brief, and so the two were combined into a single Sunday morning service.[4]

This theory may well be correct. However, we also need to remember that Jewish festive meals could likewise include an informal ministry of the word, with readings, songs and discourse, and that there are signs in the New Testament of eucharistic celebrations that already

---

[3] *First Apology* 67.3–5 (*PEER*, pp. 29–30).

[4] On the choice of Sunday as the Christian day of worship, see below, pp. 83–6.

had elements of this sort attached to them. There is, for example, the account of the appearance of the risen Jesus to the disciples on the road to Emmaus, where he interprets the Scriptures to them before breaking bread with them (Luke 24.13–35), which is often seen as reflecting the regular pattern of eucharistic worship known to the author. There is the assembly at Troas, where Paul preaches at length and then breaks bread with the company (Acts 20.7–12). And there is also the mention in 1 Corinthians 14.26 of 'a hymn, a lesson, a revelation, a tongue, or an interpretation' contributed to common worship by the participants, which may refer to the same occasion as the meal referred to earlier in 1 Corinthians 11. So the later practice may be as much an expansion and formalization of this earlier tradition as a fusion of a synagogue-style gathering with the remnants of the meal ritual.

But even more important than the change in the rite's structure is the effect that the change in practice would have had on what the Christians experienced. There is a world of difference between enjoying companionship around a table at an evening meal and rising early in the morning to engage in a hasty ritual act before setting out for work. Yet even so, something of the close sense of community which had been engendered by the meal still managed to survive in this new form of the Eucharist. We may note, for instance, how Justin stresses the fact that there is a single assembly 'in one place of all who live in town or country', and how he similarly attaches importance to the assent of the people in the 'Amen' at the end of the eucharistic prayer, and to the inclusion of the absent members in the act of communion. In an earlier account that he gives of a Eucharist following the baptism of new members, Justin also mentions that the common prayers of the people were concluded with the exchange of a kiss on the lips (above, p. 15) – which would have been an unusually intimate action in that culture for those who were unrelated to one another, but which we find in other later sources as a regular part of the eucharistic rite symbolizing the familial relationship that Christians felt they shared with one another.

7

Anamnesis and epiclesis:
the eucharistic prayer

Although the precise wording of the Jewish meal prayers over the bread and the cup had probably not yet become firmly fixed during the first century, there was a long established tradition of such prayers of blessing within Judaism, reaching back to Old Testament times. According to this tradition, it would not have been the bread or the wine that was the object of the blessing, but God. In Jewish prayers God was blessed or thanked for what he had done, in rescuing the people from slavery in Egypt, in giving them the promised land and the law to direct their lives, in bringing forth food from the earth and creating the fruit of the vine, and so on. Thus the prayers involved the remembrance (or in Greek, *anamnesis*) of God's mighty works.

In the Jewish world, remembrance was not understood as a purely mental activity. For example, when the penitent thief asked Jesus to 'remember me when you come into your kingdom' (Luke 23.42), he did not expect Jesus merely to think about him, but to act, to do something about his situation. Thus, the worshippers' recalling in prayer of what God had done was not simply nostalgia for the past but led naturally to their petition that God in turn would remember his people, that is, that he would continue to act in the present and the future in similar ways. Because God's nature was constant and unchanging, the one who had liberated Israel from slavery in Egypt would surely also free them from their present sufferings. Hence Jewish prayers of remembrance frequently led into a second half that involved invocation (in Greek, *epiclesis*), calling upon God to continue his saving work among them.

This helps us to comprehend what might have been meant by the saying 'Do this in remembrance of me' (1 Corinthians 11.24, 25). It cannot have been intended to initiate some novel ritual practice that the early Christians would not otherwise have done, but was instead a direction that when they performed the customary meal ritual, they were to do so in future with a new meaning – as a remembrance of Jesus. Although scholars have often disputed whether this should be understood as 'do this in order that you may remember me' or instead as 'do this in order that God may remember me', the two ideas are really closely connected in Jewish thought and prayer. The disciples' act of remembering Jesus in their eucharistic meals would inevitably have included calling upon God also to remember and to act. We would expect, therefore, that Christianized forms of the Jewish table-prayers would include some recalling of what God had done in Jesus Christ, and some petition for God to bring to completion his saving purposes.

The *Didache*

The New Testament itself does not contain any complete prayer texts of this kind, although there are perhaps hints of them here and there. However, the ancient church order known as the *Didache* has preserved some Christian meal prayers that do what we would expect – recall and request.

About the thanksgiving: give thanks thus: First, about the cup:
We give thanks to you, our Father for the holy vine of your child David, which you have made known to us through your child Jesus; glory to you for evermore.
And about the broken bread:
We give thanks to you, our Father, for the life and knowledge which you have made known to us through your child Jesus; glory to you for evermore. As this broken bread was scattered over the mountains and when brought together became one, so let your Church be brought together from the ends of the earth into your kingdom; for yours are the glory and the power through Jesus Christ for evermore.
But let no one eat or drink of your thanksgiving but those who have been baptized in the name of the Lord. For about this also the Lord has said, 'Do not give what is holy to the dogs.'
And after you have had your fill, give thanks thus:
We give thanks to you, holy Father, for your holy Name which you have enshrined in our hearts, and for the knowledge and faith and

immortality which you have made known to us through your child Jesus; glory to you for evermore.

You, Almighty Master, created all things for the sake of your Name and gave food and drink to humankind for their enjoyment, that they might give you thanks; but to us you have granted spiritual food and drink and eternal life through your child Jesus. Above all we give you thanks because you are mighty; glory to you for evermore. Amen.

Remember, Lord, your Church, to deliver it from all evil and to perfect it in your love, and bring it together from the four winds, now sanctified, into your kingdom which you have prepared for it; for yours are the power and the glory for evermore. Amen.

> May grace come and this world pass away.
> Hosanna to the God of David.
> If any be holy, let him come; if any be not, let him repent.
> Marana tha. Amen.
> *But allow the prophets to give thanks as they wish.*[1]

These prayers have many similarities with what eventually became the standard Jewish table prayers, and so suggest the sort of thing that early Jewish Christians might well have used at their eucharistic meals. We should note in particular the themes of communion and eschatological fulfilment underlying the emphasis in the *epiclesis* parts of the prayers on the Church being gathered together and brought into the kingdom.

The instruction at the end that prophets might use their own words instead of these texts is echoed in Justin Martyr's statement that the president 'sends up prayers and thanksgivings according to his ability' (above, p. 47) and points to the widespread tradition that those responsible for leading eucharistic worship usually had freedom to improvise their prayers within the limits of the accepted conventions of their local community. It was only in the fourth century that written prayers became more common, therefore, and this explains the dearth of texts older than that. However, there are a few examples from this later period that may well embody a pattern of prayer used in earlier times, even if they have undergone some later expansion or modification.

---

[1] *Didache* 9–10 (*PEER*, pp. 23–4).

The Strasbourg Papyrus

One of these, written on papyrus and now preserved at Strasbourg, comes originally from Egypt. Although it only exists in a fragmentary form, it seems to be an early (perhaps even third-century) version of what later became the standard eucharistic prayer of the Coptic Church, the Anaphora of St Mark:

to bless (you) . . . (night) and day . . . (you who made) heaven (and) all that is in (it, the earth and what is on earth,) seas and rivers and (all that is) in (them); (you) who made human beings (according to your) own image and likeness. You made everything through your wisdom, the light (of?) your true Son, our Lord and Savior Jesus Christ; giving thanks through him to you with him and the Holy Spirit, we offer the reasonable sacrifice and this bloodless service, which all the nations offer you, 'from sunrise to sunset,' from south to north, (for) your 'name is great among all the nations, and in every place incense is offered to your holy name and a pure sacrifice.'

Over this sacrifice and offering we pray and beseech you, remember your holy and only Catholic Church, all your peoples and all your flocks. Provide the peace which is from heaven in all our hearts, and grant us also the peace of this life. The . . . of the land peaceful things towards us, and towards your (holy) name, the prefect of the province, the army, the princes, councils . . .

[About one-third of a page is lacking here, and what survives is in places too fragmentary to be restored.]

(for seedtime and) harvest . . . preserve, for the poor of (your) people, for all of us who call upon (your) name, for all who hope in you. Give rest to the souls of those who have fallen asleep; remember those of whom we make mention today, both those whose names we say (and) whose we do not say . . . (Remember) our orthodox fathers and bishops everywhere; and grant us to have a part and lot with the fair . . . of your holy prophets, apostles, and martyrs. Receive(?) (through) their entreaties (these prayers); grant them through our Lord, through whom be glory to you to the ages of ages. (PEER, pp. 53–4)

While this text looks much less like the Jewish forms than the *Didache* prayers were, because it apparently arose in a Gentile context, it still preserves the basic elements of *anamnesis* and *epiclesis*. New features here are the introduction of a reference to sacrifice in the middle, citing Malachi 1.11 and effectively creating a tripartite structure that we shall also see in other prayers, and the extension of the petitionary part of the prayer into a full range of intercessions for all sorts of people rather than simply focusing upon the communion of the participants and their admission to the heavenly banquet. These two developments appear to be related to one another, and we shall say more about them in a later chapter.

The *Apostolic Tradition*

Neither of the texts we have looked at so far concentrates on the saving effects of the death of Christ nor contains an explicit reference to the Last Supper, as we might have expected. Instead, the Strasbourg Papyrus seems primarily concerned with the theme of creation, and the *Didache* prayers with the revelation brought by Jesus. However, this was not true of all early eucharistic prayers. The prayer in the *Apostolic Tradition* attributed to Hippolytus centres much more on the theme of redemption, and makes only a passing reference to creation. Although we do not know with any certainty its place and date of composition, it shows similarities of structure with prayers of West Syrian origin known from the fourth century onwards and so it may well have come from there.

Then the deacons shall present the offering to him [the bishop]; and he laying his hands on it with all the presbytery, shall say, giving thanks:
The Lord be with you.
And all shall say:
And with your spirit.
Up with your hearts.
We have (them) with the Lord.
Let us give thanks to the Lord.
It is fitting and right.
And then he shall continue thus:
We render thanks to you, O God, through your beloved child Jesus Christ, whom in these last times you sent to us as a savior and redeemer and angel of your will; who is your inseparable Word, through whom you made all things, and in whom you were well pleased. You sent him from heaven into a virgin's womb; and conceived in the womb, he was made flesh and was manifested as your Son, being born of the Holy Spirit and the Virgin. Fulfilling your will and gaining for you a holy people, he stretched out his hands when he should suffer, that he might release from suffering those who have believed in you.

Anamnesis

53

And when he was betrayed to voluntary suffering that he might destroy death, and break the bonds of the devil, and tread down hell, and shine upon the righteous, and fix a term, and manifest the resurrection, he took bread and gave thanks to you, saying, 'Take, eat; this is my body, which shall be broken for you.' Likewise also the cup, saying, 'This is my blood, which is shed for you; when you do this, you make my remembrance.'

Remembering, therefore, his death and resurrection, we offer to you the bread and the cup, giving you thanks because you have held us worthy to stand before you and minister to you. And we ask that you would send your Holy Spirit upon the offering of your holy Church; that, gathering her into one, you would grant to all who receive the holy things (to receive) for the fullness of the Holy Spirit for the strengthening of faith in truth; that we may praise and glorify you through your child Jesus Christ, through whom be glory and honor to you, to the Father and the Son, with the Holy Spirit, in your holy Church, both now and to the ages of ages.   (*PEER*, pp. 34–5)

All our other evidence indicates that the account of the Last Supper (or narrative of institution, as it is called by liturgical scholars) gradually began to appear in eucharistic prayers from about the middle of the fourth century onwards. Hence, it seems likely that at least that part of the above text was added to the prayer around that period, especially as it seems to interrupt the series of thanksgivings for redemption and the calling of the people of God. Some scholars have argued that the petition for the sending of the Holy Spirit is also a later addition, because its language is more consistent with fourth-century thought (as also is the trinitarian ascription at the end). Once again, we will consider further both these matters in a subsequent chapter. What is thus left as the older nucleus of the prayer has the familiar pattern of *anamnesis* and *epiclesis*, with a brief statement of offering between the two, as in the Strasbourg Papyrus. While the first part has a stronger Christological emphasis than we saw in the other prayers, the second part retains the primitive focus on petition for the fruits of communion.

Later developments

The late fourth century saw not only the gradual emergence in nearly all eucharistic prayers of secondary elements of the sort that we can see in the prayer from the *Apostolic Tradition* and of extensive intercession similar to that in the Strasbourg Papyrus, but also the widespread introduction of an expression of praise of the Creator culminating in the angelic hymn, 'Holy, holy, holy, Lord God of hosts . . .', an adaptation of Isaiah 6.3 found in the Jewish synagogue liturgy. There are signs to suggest that this unit may have formed a part of some Egyptian eucharistic prayers from an earlier date and spread from there to other regions of the world in the general process of assimilation and liturgical standardization that is characteristic of orthodox Christianity after the Council of Nicaea in 325. Because all these elements were not always inserted in exactly the same place in the various local prayer patterns, the process resulted in quite different structures of eucharistic prayer in the different regions of East and West, and these variations persisted in later centuries.

8

Holy food

There is another strand of thought present in the New Testament which would be strongly developed in later centuries, and that focuses not on the meal as event, but on the bread and wine themselves as spiritual food. We can perhaps even see this emerging in the difference between the remembered words of Jesus over the cup of wine in Paul and in Mark. Paul recalls the words as being 'this cup is the new covenant in my blood' (1 Corinthians 11.25), suggesting a vision of the Eucharist as effective action, the shared meal sealing a covenant between God and those partaking of it which had been made by the shedding of the blood of Jesus, just as in the Old Testament covenants were sealed in sacrificial blood. Mark's version, on the other hand, speaks more directly of the wine as 'This is my blood of the covenant' (14.24), which seems to imply that the presence of the Lord was attached to the food rather than to the meal event. This way of thinking is even more clearly revealed in the 'I am the bread of life' discourse of John 6.

Alongside their continuing understanding of the Eucharist as a communal action, therefore, the writings of the second and third centuries also develop this way of thinking. Thus, for example, one of the prayers in the *Didache* speaks of the gift of 'spiritual food and drink' (above, p. 51); and Justin Martyr provides the earliest example of the food rather than the rite being called *eucharistia*, and goes on to say:

> We do not receive these things as common bread or common drink; but just as our Savior Jesus Christ, being incarnate through the word of God, took flesh and blood for our salvation, so too we have been taught that the food over which thanks have been given by a word of prayer which is from him, from which our flesh and blood are fed by transformation, is both the flesh and blood of that incarnate Jesus.[1]

---

[1] *First Apology* 66.1–2 (*PEER*, p. 29).

Justin is also the first to describe the custom of the bread and wine from the Sunday Eucharist being taken to those unable to be present at it (*First Apology* 65.5; 67.5), while Tertullian at the end of the second century refers to those present at the celebration also taking bread home for consumption there during the week (*Ad uxorem* 2.5; cf. also *De oratione* 19). Both these practices continue to be attested by later sources, sometimes with bread alone, and sometimes with wine as well, though difficulties in transporting and storing the latter safely made it less common. Their origin almost certainly lies in the desire mentioned above (p. 43) to ensure that the poor in the Christian community might be adequately fed, and so enough would have been given to them by these means to help satisfy their physical hunger every day. Later, when communion was reduced to token amounts, it would have continued to be shared with those who were absent and also taken home by some believers as a way of feeding spiritually on Christ each day. Indeed, it seems likely that the transition of eucharistic celebrations from evenings to mornings itself emerged out of a custom of distributing leftovers at that time to those unable to have been present at an evening meal the previous day. Tertullian, for instance, at the end of the second century seems familiar with the existence of both an evening supper assembly and the distribution of communion in the mornings, an apparent halfway stage in this development.[2] Yet the abstraction of the eucharistic elements from the context of the meal in these various ways would inevitably have served to encourage them to be thought of as being special in themselves.

As the quotation above from Justin shows, early Christians were happy to use highly 'realistic' language about the bread and wine, affirming that they were truly the body and blood of Christ. This appears to have arisen in order to counteract heretical claims that Christ was not truly human and did not really suffer and die on the cross. Ignatius of Antioch in the early second century, for example, says that some 'abstain from eucharist and prayer because they do not acknowledge the eucharist to be the flesh of our Saviour Jesus Christ which suffered for our sins and which the Father raised by his

---

[2] *Apologeticum* 39; *De corona* 3; *De oratione* 19. See Andrew B. McGowan, 'Rethinking Agape and Eucharist in Early North African Christianity', *Studia Liturgica* 34 (2004), pp. 165–76.

goodness' (*To the Smyrnaeans* 7.1). Thus eucharistic realism arose out of Christological realism. On the other hand, later Christian theologians appear to have recognized the possibility that such language might be misinterpreted and so more cautious terms, such as 'figure', 'sign', 'symbol' or 'type', began to appear. Cyril of Jerusalem, for instance, states that Christ's 'body has been bestowed on you in the form (Greek: *typos*) of bread, and his blood in the form (*typos*) of wine', and that communicants 'taste not bread and wine but the sign (*antitypon*) of Christ's body and blood'.[3] Similarly, Ambrose of Milan testifies that the eucharistic prayer of his church spoke of the elements as being 'the figure (Latin: *figura*) of the body and blood of our Lord Jesus Christ'.[4] We should not make too much of these differences in language, however. In the ancient world a sign or symbol was not thought of as being something quite different from the reality which it represented, but on the contrary was understood as participating in some way in that reality itself. Moreover, the same writers who use 'symbolic' language also usually have no hesitation in using more 'realistic' language on occasion. Thus Cyril can state quite unequivocally: 'Do not, then, regard the bread and wine as nothing but bread and wine, for they are the body and blood of Christ as the Master himself has proclaimed.'[5]

Consecration

The identification of the bread and wine as in some sense the body and blood of Christ inevitably raised the theological question as to how these ordinary things became this holy food. Justin Martyr's answer to this question, as we have seen earlier in this chapter, appears to have been that it was the result of thanks having been given over it 'by a word of prayer which is from him'. However, the original Greek here is ambiguous, and so it would be equally possible to translate the phrase as 'by a prayer of the word that is from him' or as 'by the prayer of the Word [*Logos*, i.e. Christ] who is from him', and what Justin means to say has been variously explained by scholars. Does the 'him' refer to God or to Christ? Is he saying that the actual

---

[3] *Mystagogical Catechesis* 4.3; 5.20 (*AIR*, pp. 86, 95).
[4] *De sacramentis* 4.21 (*AIR*, p. 136).
[5] *Mystagogical Catechesis* 4.6 (*AIR*, p. 87).

form of words used comes from Christ or God, or that the prayer includes an invocation of the *Logos* on the bread and wine, or just that the prayer has its origin in God's word? The last seems the most likely, especially as there is a similar statement in 1 Timothy 4.4–5, that 'nothing is to be rejected if it is received with thanksgiving; for then it is consecrated by the word of God and prayer'.

Later, however, the emphasis begins to fall less on the prayer as thanksgiving and more on its function as invocation – indeed the word *epiclesis* comes to be used to designate the whole prayer. Thus Irenaeus in the late second century says that 'the bread . . . when it receives the invocation of God is no longer common bread, but the eucharist, consisting of two realities, the earthly and the heavenly'.[6] As a result of this way of thinking, the language of the second half of eucharistic prayers also began to change and develop. As we have seen, at first this petitionary element had tended to focus on the communicants themselves. Eventually, however, petitions began to appear which requested God to act in relation to the bread and wine as well as, or in some cases instead of, the congregation. Sometimes God was asked to send the second person of the Trinity – the *Logos* – and sometimes it was the Holy Spirit who was called down. This was because Christians at first did not distinguish as sharply between the two as they did after the fourth-century trinitarian debates. They often thought of the Holy Spirit as being the spirit of the risen Christ, and so tended to use the two terms somewhat interchangeably.

Thus, in the eucharistic prayer attributed to Sarapion, the mid-fourth-century bishop of Thmuis in Egypt, God is asked: 'let your holy Word come on this bread, O God of truth, that the bread may become body of the Word; and on this cup, that the cup may become blood of the Truth; and make all who partake . . .' (*PEER*, pp. 77–8). On the other hand, the petition in the eucharistic prayer of the *Apostolic Tradition* asks God to 'send your Holy Spirit upon the offering of your holy Church' (above, p. 54). While some scholars judge this to be a fourth-century addition to the text, others believe that 'the offering' here refers to the action, the eucharistic sacrifice of praise, rather than more narrowly to the elements alone. Whatever the truth of

---

[6] *Adversus haereses* 4.18.5; English translation from David N. Power, *Irenaeus of Lyons on Baptism and Eucharist* (Grove Books, Nottingham 1991), p. 15.

that particular case, it was only after the fourth-century debates that orthodox churches of the East began to attach great importance to the inclusion of an explicit *epiclesis* of the Holy Spirit on the eucharistic elements.

We can also see a gradual development in what the Spirit is expected to do in connection with the bread and wine. At first, imprecise verbs like 'bless' and 'sanctify' are found, as in the ancient East Syrian eucharistic prayer of Addai and Mari: 'may your Holy Spirit, Lord, come and rest on this offering of your servants, and bless and sanctify it' (*PEER*, p. 43). The fourth-century prayer of St Basil, however, adds the Greek verb *anadeiknumi* ('show forth'): 'And we, sinners and unworthy and wretched, pray you, our God, in adoration that in the good pleasure of your goodness your Holy Spirit may descend upon us and upon these gifts that have been set before you, and may sanctify them and show them forth as holy of holies'.[7] Similarly, Theodore of Mopsuestia explains that the bishop entreats God 'that the Holy Spirit may come and that grace may descend from on high on to the bread and wine that have been offered, so showing us that the memorial of immortality is truly the body and blood of our Lord'.[8] This reflects a shift towards what might be called an 'epiphany' understanding of consecration, in which the Spirit is invoked on the community and on the gifts in order that the presence of Christ may be revealed in them.

On the other hand, a number of other fourth-century sources use language about eucharistic consecration that suggests instead the idea of a change or conversion in the elements of bread and wine rather than a revealing of what was hidden. Cyril of Jerusalem, for example, implies that the eucharistic prayer known to him asked God to send the Holy Spirit to 'make' the elements the body and blood of Christ,[9] and we have already seen the verb 'become' used in this way in the eucharistic prayer of Sarapion. Even stronger language is found in the eucharistic prayer which is attributed to John Chrysostom, although first known to us from an eighth-century manuscript:

---

[7] *PEER*, p. 71; but the translation 'make them holy of holies' has been amended here in order to make its true meaning clearer.

[8] *Baptismal Homily* 5.12 (*AIR*, p. 233).

[9] *Mystagogical Catechesis* 5.7 (*AIR*, p. 92).

we pray and beseech and entreat you, send down your Holy Spirit on
us and on these gifts set forth; and make this bread the precious body
of your Christ, changing it by your Holy Spirit, Amen; and that which
is in this cup the precious blood of your Christ, changing it by your
holy Spirit, Amen.   (*PEER*, p. 133)

In the writings of Ambrose in the West in the fourth century we
find similar language about a change in the eucharistic elements.
In contrast to the Eastern sources, however, Ambrose understands
this to be effected not by an invocation of the Holy Spirit (which
seems to have been absent from eucharistic prayers in his tradition)
but rather through the recitation of the words of Christ in the
narrative of institution, which was already a part of the eucharistic
prayer in Milan where he was bishop:

> How can something which is bread be the body of Christ? Well, by
> what words is the consecration effected, and whose words are they?
> The words of the Lord Jesus. All that is said before are the words of
> the priest: praise is offered to God, the prayer is offered up, petitions
> are made for the people, for kings, for all others. But when the moment
> comes for bringing the most holy sacrament into being, the priest does
> not use his own words any longer: he uses the words of Christ. Therefore,
> it is Christ's word that brings this sacrament into being. What is the
> word of Christ? It is the word by which all things were made . . .[10]

While Ambrose views the source of consecration as being the biblical
'word of God/Christ', later doctrine in the West would attribute eucharistic consecration more narrowly to the recitation of the dominical
words in the institution narrative, and thus distinguish itself from
Eastern Christian theology, which continued to attach consecratory
significance to the *epiclesis* of the Holy Spirit.

---

[10] *De sacramentis* 5.14 (*AIR*, pp. 132–3).

9

'The bloodless sacrifice'

The notion of sacrifice as the normal means of human interaction with the divine was fundamental to all religions in the ancient world, and Israel was no exception. In most forms of Israelite sacrifice an animal or grain offering was handed over completely to God and consumed by fire, the sweet smell of it being thought of as ascending to God for his pleasure. But in what are known as communion-sacrifices, part of what was offered was returned to those who had offered it to be eaten by them, so that in effect they shared a sacred meal with God as a sign of his acceptance of them through the sacrificial act. The most important of these communion-sacrifices was the annual Passover celebration. Although in origin the Passover had been a nomadic spring ritual intended to secure fecundity for the flock, it had become for the Israelite people a remembrance of their deliverance by God from slavery in Egypt. Following the prescriptions in Exodus 12, on the day of the festival each family was supposed to take a lamb and offer it for sacrifice in the Temple at Jerusalem, and then consume it together in a ritual meal.

In the Christian tradition the idea of worship as a sacrifice was retained, but the material offering of animals replaced by a more 'spiritualized' or 'bloodless' concept. Although St Paul had used the image of the communion-sacrifice in order to express the source of the unity of those participating in the eucharistic meal in 1 Corinthians 10.16–17 ('The cup of blessing which we bless, is it not a communion in the blood of Christ? The bread which we break, is it not a communion in the body of Christ? Because there is one bread, we who are many are one body, for we all partake of the one bread'), this biblical model for the rite tended to fade away, with the result that receiving communion eventually ceased to be thought of as an essential part of the action. Nevertheless, as we shall see, the concept of sacrifice continued to influence Christian thought and practice in several different ways.

'Pure' sacrifice: the offering of life and of praise

The roots of this idea can already be seen within first-century Judaism. The writings of Philo of Alexandria, who was strongly influenced by Stoic and Platonic philosophy, reveal a vision of the only sacrifice worthy of God as being that of a pure mind and soul offering itself to God; and the sectarian Jewish community at Qumran similarly regarded the offering of a life of virtue and of words of divine praise, 'the fruit of our lips' (Hosea 14.2), as an acceptable temporary substitute for the Temple cult, from which they had separated themselves on the grounds that it had become corrupt.

Thus, in the New Testament we find, for example, St Paul exhorting his readers 'to present your bodies as a living sacrifice, holy and acceptable to God, which is your spiritual worship' (Romans 12.1). Similarly, the author of the Epistle to the Hebrews, while on the one hand insisting that Christ's own oblation of himself has put an end to the need for propitiatory sacrifice once and for all (Hebrews 10.10–18), can still call for Christians to offer to God both praise (citing Hosea) and a life of love for others: 'Through him [i.e. Jesus] then let us continually offer up a sacrifice of praise to God, that is, the fruit of lips that acknowledge his name. Do not neglect to do good and to share what you have, for such sacrifices are pleasing to God' (Hebrews 13.15–16).

It is not surprising, therefore, that in Christian writings of the second and third centuries all prayer, and not just the Eucharist alone, was understood as constituting a sacrifice of praise offered to God.[1] Nevertheless, it was inevitable that among all the acts of worship offered to God by Christians the Eucharist should come to be viewed as the pre-eminent sacrifice of praise. Indeed, it was a standard part of their polemic against the Jews that Christians were the ones who truly fulfilled what they understood to be a prophecy in Malachi 1.11 ('from the rising of the sun to its setting my name is great among the nations, and in every place incense is offered to my name, and a pure offering') because they offered the Eucharist to praise and glorify God in every place, while the Jews had only offered their sacrifices in the Temple in Jerusalem.[2]

---

[1] See below, p. 79.
[2] See, for example, Justin Martyr, *Dialogue with Trypho* 41 (*PEER*, p. 27).

An early example of this way of thinking occurs in the *Didache*, which instructs Christians to come together on the Lord's day, 'break bread, and give thanks, having first confessed your transgressions, that your sacrifice may be pure'. Those who have quarrelled must also be reconciled to one another before joining in the celebration 'that your sacrifice may not be defiled'.[3] Here the 'pure offering' is seen as requiring purity of life as well as words of praise and thanksgiving, a message that had been articulated by the Old Testament prophets and reiterated in the teaching of Jesus (see, for example, Mark 7.1–23). It is this idea of the Eucharist as the sacrifice of praise that we find conveyed in the eucharistic prayer of the Strasbourg Papyrus with its explicit quotation from Malachi, which we looked at in a previous chapter (above, p. 52), and it recurs in more subtly expressed forms in other liturgical texts.

Gift-sacrifice: the offering of bread and wine

The transition in the primary understanding of the Eucharist from 'sacred meal' to 'holy food' also had an effect upon Christians' understanding of the sort of sacrifice they thought was offered in the Eucharist. While the idea that it was the act of praise that they were offering to God persisted in both liturgical texts and theological writings in later times, there emerged alongside it the notion that the bread and wine constituted the Christian offering. We can see this concept already in Justin Martyr. While affirming that 'prayers and thanksgivings made by those worthy are the only sacrifices that are perfect and well-pleasing to God', at the same time Justin linked these with the offering of the 'bread of the thanksgiving and likewise the cup of the thanksgiving' as constituting the fulfilment of the material oblations of the Old Testament.[4] The fact that the worshippers themselves brought the bread and wine with them from their homes to be used in the Eucharist (just as they had earlier contributed the food and drink for the full eucharistic meal) would have further encouraged the idea that these elements formed the substance of the sacrifice.

---

[3] *Didache* 14 (*PEER*, p. 24).
[4] *Dialogue with Trypho* 41.3; 117.2 (*PEER*, pp. 27–8).

This concept was given a unique twist by Irenaeus of Lyons in the late second century, who saw the eucharistic oblation of bread and wine as symbolic of the offering of the first-fruits of creation, which had been mandated in the Old Testament: 'The Lord gave directions to his disciples to offer first-fruits to God from God's own creatures, not as though God stood in need of them, but that they themselves may be neither unfruitful nor ungrateful.'[5] It is clear that here the prime purpose of the offering is seen to be the spiritual benefit that the act brings to those who perform it.

The notion that the bread and wine were the material of the Christian oblation also found its way into liturgical texts. In the *Apostolic Tradition*, for example, they are described as 'the offering', and the eucharistic prayer explicitly states: 'we offer to you the bread and the cup . . .' (above, p. 54), expressions that recur in other liturgical texts.

Memorial-sacrifice: the remembrance of Christ's self-offering

So far we have been considering themes that led to the understanding of the Eucharist as being a sacrifice in its own right, as it were. Christians of course recognized that they had been constituted into a priesthood (1 Peter 2.5, 9; Revelation 1.6; 5.10; 20.6) and made worthy to offer sacrifice to God only through Jesus Christ, but the ways of thinking outlined above did not make any direct connection between the sacrificial nature of the eucharistic rite or its elements and the sacrificial character of Christ's death.

Nevertheless, from early times the Eucharist was understood as a memorial of Christ's sacrifice. This is a fundamental strand in the New Testament tradition. Both Paul and the synoptic Gospels associate the origin of the Eucharist with the Last Supper, which they understand as a Passover meal with its inevitable sacrificial overtones, and although they differ as to the exact words of Jesus over the bread and cup, they all record them as pointing to a sacrificial

---

[5] *Adversus haereses* 4.17.5; see also 4.18.1. English translation from David N. Power, *Irenaeus of Lyons on Baptism and Eucharist* (Grove Books, Nottingham 1991), p. 15.

interpretation of the act: 'this is my body/my body which is for you'; 'blood of the covenant, which is poured out for many/new covenant in my blood'. Indeed, Paul goes on to identify the Christian rite explicitly as a memorial of Christ's passion: 'For as often as you eat this bread and drink the cup, you proclaim the Lord's death until he comes' (1 Corinthians 11.26).

In the second century Justin Martyr made a connection between the oblation of the bread and the memorial of Christ's passion: 'The offering of fine flour . . . which was handed down to be offered by those who were cleansed from leprosy, was a type of the bread of the thanksgiving, which our Lord Jesus Christ handed down to us to do for the remembrance of the suffering which he suffered for those who are cleansed in their souls from all wickedness of men, so that we might give thanks to God.'[6] In the same way, the phrase about the offering of the bread and cup in the eucharistic prayer of the *Apostolic Tradition* quoted earlier in this chapter follows directly upon the narrative of the Last Supper and is linked with remembrance, here extended to include the resurrection as well: 'Remembering, therefore, his death and resurrection, we offer to you the bread and the cup . . .'.

Once again, other eucharistic prayers would follow this lead. In all these instances, therefore, the idea of the remembrance of Christ's sacrificial death is being combined with the pre-existing notion of the eucharist itself as a sacrifice to create what we might perhaps describe as the concept of the rite as a memorial-sacrifice.

The writings of Cyprian, the third-century bishop of Carthage, may possibly mark a further significant change in this idea:

> For if Jesus Christ, our Lord and God, is himself the chief priest of God the Father, and has first offered himself a sacrifice to the Father, and has commanded this to be done in commemoration of himself, certainly that priest truly discharges the office of Christ, who imitates that which Christ did; and he then offers a true and full sacrifice in the Church to God the Father, when he proceeds to offer it according to what he sees Christ himself to have offered.[7]

---

[6] *Dialogue with Trypho* 41.1; see also 117.3 (*PEER*, pp. 27–8).

[7] *Epistulae* 63.14; English translation from Alexander Roberts and James Donaldson (eds), *The Ante-Nicene Fathers*, vol. 5 (Charles Scribner's Sons, New York 1919), p. 362.

Some scholars would interpret Cyprian as saying that in the Eucharist the priest (by which he means the bishop) offers the same sacrifice that Christ offered on the cross, i.e. that the bishop 'offers Christ'. While this is certainly the first place where the bishop is said to 'discharge the office of Christ', other scholars think that the image should not be taken quite so literally but means no more than something like: 'just as Christ offered himself as a sacrifice, so too does the bishop offer the Church's sacrifice in memory of him'.

Whatever Cyprian may have meant, however, some later Christian writers unquestionably use language that does identify the Church's sacrificial act very closely indeed with the sacrifice of Christ. Thus, for example, Cyril of Jerusalem states, 'we offer Christ who has been slain for our sins';[8] and Gregory of Nazianzus says that 'you sacrifice the Master's body and blood with bloodless knife' (*Epistulae* 171). John Chrysostom, however, in one of his homilies struggled between this way of talking and the conviction that there was only one sacrifice of Christ, even though there were many celebrations of the Eucharist:

> Do we not offer every day? We offer indeed, but making a remembrance of his death, and this [remembrance] is one and not many. How is it one and not many? In as much as that [sacrifice] was once for all offered, [and] carried into the holy of holies. This is a figure of that [sacrifice] and this remembrance of that. For we always offer the same, not one sheep now and tomorrow another, but always the same thing, so that the sacrifice is one. And yet by this reasoning, since the offering is made in many places, are there many Christs? But Christ is one everywhere, being complete here and complete there also, one body. As then while offered in many places, he is one body and not many bodies, so also [he is] one sacrifice. He is our high priest, who offered the sacrifice that cleanses us. That we offer now also, which was then offered, which cannot be exhausted. This is done in remembrance of what was then done. For (saith he) 'do this in remembrance of me.' It is not another sacrifice, as the high priest, but we offer always the same, or rather we perform a remembrance of a sacrifice.[9]

---

[8] *Mystagogical Catechesis* 5.10 (*AIR*, p. 94).

[9] *In epistulam ad Hebraeos* 17.6; English translation from Philip Schaff (ed.), *A Select Library of the Nicene and Post-Nicene Fathers of the Christian Church* (T&T Clark, Edinburgh 1886–1900), vol. 14, p. 449.

Ancient liturgical texts themselves, on the other hand, were much more conservative in their language, and spoke rather in terms of celebrating the memorial of Christ's sacrifice. While a very close relationship was seen between Christ's sacrifice and the Church's offering, some distinction between the two was also maintained.

Propitiatory sacrifice

We saw earlier that a petitionary element seems to have been integral to the basic structure of the earliest eucharistic prayers, and that it appears to have focused on praying for the gathering together of the communicants into one body in readiness for the coming of God's kingdom. Once the theme of sacrifice had made its way into eucharistic prayers, it would have been natural for some connection to be made between the act of offering and these petitions. Christians would have been reminded of other kinds of Old Testament sacrifices in which offerings were made in the hope of propitiating God's justifiable anger against sinful human conduct and averting divine punishment, or with the intention of securing other benefits. Hence, it is not surprising to find that the scope of these petitions begins to be enlarged.

The ancient East Syrian prayer of Addai and Mari, for example, prays for 'remission of debts, forgiveness of sins' as well as for 'the great hope of resurrection from the dead, and new life in the kingdom of heaven, with all who have been pleasing in your sight' (*PEER*, p. 43). The Strasbourg Papyrus, as we saw in a previous chapter (above, p. 52), included a very wide range of objects of intercession which it explicitly connected with the Church's offering: 'Over this sacrifice and offering we pray and beseech you, remember your holy and only Catholic Church, all your peoples and all your flocks.' Similarly, in describing the pattern of eucharistic prayer with which he was familiar, Cyril of Jerusalem in the fourth century said:

> Then, when the spiritual sacrifice – this worship without blood – has been completed, we beg God over the sacrifice of propitiation for general peace among the churches, for the right order of the world, for the kings, for soldiers and allies, for the sick and the afflicted, and in short we all make entreaty and offer this sacrifice for all who need help. Next we recall those who have gone to rest before us, and first of all the patriarchs, prophets, apostles and martyrs, so that God may

listen to our appeal through their prayers and representations. After that, we pray on behalf of the holy fathers and bishops and in general for all amongst us already gone to their rest, for we believe that these souls will obtain the greatest help if we make our prayers for them when the holy and most awesome sacrifice has been set on the altar.[10]

This idea led both to greatly expanded intercession in eucharistic prayers everywhere and also, in Western Christianity, to the emergence of special celebrations of the Eucharist on weekdays with the intention of securing some particular benefit. One of the earliest forms of this was a celebration on the anniversary of a person's death so as to intercede for the repose of his or her soul, a practice which has its roots long before the fourth century.

---

[10] *Mystagogical Catechesis* 5.8–9 (*AIR*, pp. 93–4).

10

'Let all mortal flesh keep silence'

The fourth century witnessed a further change in eucharistic practice that was nearly as profound as the change brought about by the disappearance of the meal. This was the emergence of an attitude of great awe and fear directed towards the eucharistic elements, together with a decline in the frequency of the reception of communion.

The introduction of the numinous

When looking at the development of Christian initiation, we saw that a major change took place in the way in which the rituals were performed after the Peace of Constantine in the fourth century. The lack of a genuine conversion experience, or even a full understanding of the significance of becoming a Christian, led to a strong dramatizing of the baptismal ceremonies in order to produce a profound emotional effect upon the candidates. Something similar also occurred in connection with the Eucharist. The members of the Church were no longer an elite group of highly committed believers, but a much larger mass of nominal converts, many of whom lacked a deep understanding of the Christian faith and an awareness of the conduct that was appropriate at its liturgical assemblies. According to John Chrysostom, for example, they pushed and pulled one another in an unruly manner during the services; they gossiped with one another; young people engaged in various kinds of mischief; and pickpockets preyed upon the crowd.[1]

In order to impress upon worshippers the solemnity of what was happening in the eucharistic rite and of the reverent behaviour appropriate for such an occasion, therefore, the style of eucharistic

[1] For references, see Robert F. Taft, '"Eastern Presuppositions" and Western Liturgical Renewal', *Antiphon* 5 (2000), pp. 10–22, here at p. 14.

celebrations underwent a significant alteration. They became much more formal and elaborate; they used such things as ceremonial actions, vesture, processions, and music in order to make an impression upon the congregation; and in word and action they stressed the majesty and transcendence of God and the divinity of Christ present in the eucharistic mystery. This last development was probably also influenced in part by the need to combat the Arian heresy, which relegated Christ to a subordinate position, and its beginnings can be seen in the opening address of the eucharistic prayer of St Basil:

> It is fitting and right, fitting and right, truly it is fitting and right, I AM, truly Lord God, existing before the ages, reigning until the ages; you dwell on high and regard what is low; you made heaven and earth and the sea and all that is in them. Father of our Lord and God and Savior Jesus Christ, through whom you made all things visible and invisible, you sit on the throne of your glory; you are adored by every holy power . . .
> (*PEER*, p. 70)

As we saw in a previous chapter (above, p. 60), the prayer also goes on to describe the worshippers as 'sinners and unworthy and wretched'.

Later prayers would develop this sort of language much further still, but at this stage it was in preaching and teaching about the Eucharist rather than in the liturgical texts themselves that the twin notes of the majesty of God and awe at Christ's presence in the sacrament were most strongly struck. This can be seen in Cyril of Jerusalem, in Theodore of Mopsuestia and most forcefully in John Chrysostom, who repeatedly speaks of the 'dreadful sacrifice', of the 'fearful moment' when the mysteries are accomplished, and of the 'terrible and awesome table' that should only be approached with fear and trembling. Cyril of Jerusalem also gives practical advice to the newly baptized on the reverent manner in which to receive communion:

> So when you come forward, do not come with arm extended or fingers parted. Make your left hand a throne for your right, since your right hand is about to welcome a king. Cup your palm and receive in it Christ's body, saying in response *Amen*. Then carefully bless your eyes with a touch of the holy body, and consume it, being careful to drop not a particle of it. For to lose any of it is clearly like losing part of

your own body ... After partaking of Christ's body, go to the chalice of his blood. Do not stretch out your hands for it. Bow your head and say *Amen* to show your homage and reverence, and sanctify yourself by partaking also of Christ's blood. While your lips are still moist with his blood, touch it with your hands and bless your eyes, forehead, and other organs of sense.[2]

We can see here that not only are the eucharistic elements to be treated with great reverence when they are consumed but they are also regarded as objects of power which can be used to confer blessing on a person's body and protect it against evil and sickness.

In short, the attitudes instilled in eucharistic worshippers at this time are well summed up in the Cherubic Hymn from the ancient Liturgy of St James, an English paraphrase of which, composed by Gerard Moultrie, is found in a number of modern hymnbooks:

> Let all mortal flesh keep silence,
> and with fear and trembling stand;
> ponder nothing earthly minded,
> for with blessing in his hand
> Christ our God to earth descendeth,
> our full homage to demand.

Non-communicating attendance

Whether this new emphasis was the cause of it or not, a significant feature of the fourth century was the tendency among a number of people to attend celebrations of the Eucharist but to abstain from receiving communion – apparently through a sense of unworthiness – for weeks or months, or sometimes for a year or more. Among fourth-century preachers, John Chrysostom was particularly vigilant in warning those who abstained not to return to the supper of the Lord without amending their way of life: 'With this, approach at all times; without it, never!' (*In epistulam ad Ephesios* 3.4). He advised those who were guilty of sin to leave the service before the eucharistic action itself began. The aim of such preaching was not to *discourage* the reception of communion, but rather to *encourage* higher standards of Christian living.

---

[2] *Mystagogical Catechesis* 5.21–2 (*AIR*, pp. 96–7).

Unfortunately, as so often happens, the results were exactly the opposite of the intentions of the preachers. Many people preferred to continue to refrain from receiving communion rather than change their behaviour. Contrary to Chrysostom's advice, they apparently stayed until the time for communion and then left the church. The ecclesiastical authorities were eventually forced to accept this practice, by making provision at the time of the communion for a formal dismissal of non-communicants so as to encourage a more orderly departure.

This practice of abstaining had a significant effect upon people's understanding of the Eucharist, since it severed the act of communion from the rest of the eucharistic action. It made it possible for people to think of the Eucharist as complete and effective without the need for them to participate in the reception of the bread and wine, and thus prepared the way for the idea that liturgy was something that the clergy did on their behalf, which ultimately did not even require their presence. We can see the beginnings of this notion in John Chrysostom. His very assertion that there are some times when there is no difference at all between the roles of priest and people is a tacit admission that there are other times when there most definitely is a difference:

> But there are occasions when there is no difference at all between the priest and those under him; for instance, when we are to partake of the awful mysteries . . . And in the prayers also, one may observe the people contributing much . . . Again, in the most awful mysteries themselves, the priest prays for the people and the people also pray for the priest; for the words 'with thy spirit' are nothing else than this. The offering of thanksgiving again is common: for neither doth he give thanks alone, but also for all the people.[3]

Eucharist as drama

For those who now began to receive communion only infrequently, the Eucharist not only ceased to be a communal action but was not even viewed as food to be eaten. Instead, it became principally an object of devotion, to be gazed on from afar. It is not surprising,

---

[3] *In epistulam secundam ad Corinthios* 18.3; English translation from Schaff (ed.), *Select Library of the Nicene and Post-Nicene Fathers*, vol. 12, pp. 365–6.

therefore, that ancient liturgical commentators began to interpret the rite in terms of a drama that unfolded before the eyes of the worshippers.

We can see this happening in the preaching of Theodore of Mopsuestia. He envisages the whole eucharistic liturgy, from the presentation of the bread and wine to the reception of communion, as a ritual allegory re-enacting the events of Jesus' passion, death, burial and resurrection. This leads him to reinterpret various liturgical actions as representing elements and moments in that story. So, for example, the bringing up of the bread and wine is no longer seen as symbolizing their offering by the people but as Christ being led to his passion; and the deacons spreading cloths on the altar 'remind us of winding-sheets'. For Theodore, the climax of the rite is at the *epiclesis* of the Holy Spirit during the eucharistic prayer, since 'this is the moment appointed for Christ our Lord to rise from the dead and pour out his grace upon us all'. The bread and wine which have until now symbolized the dead body of Jesus become his risen body. Finally, the breaking of the bread that follows the prayer symbolizes Christ's sharing of himself in his various resurrection appearances so that everyone had been able to come to him, just as the communicants were now able to do.[4]

---

[4] *Baptismal Homilies* 4.25–6; 5.11–12; 5.17–18 (*AIR*, pp. 216–17, 233–4, 236–7).

Part 3

LITURGICAL TIME

In this final section we will look at the ways that the early Christians used the various cyclical patterns of time with which they were familiar – the day, the week and the year – in order to give expression to different aspects of their beliefs.

Suggestions for further reading

In addition to works cited in notes, the following are recommended:

Paul F. Bradshaw, *Daily Prayer in the Early Church* (SPCK, London 1981; Oxford University Press, New York 1982; reprinted Wipf & Stock, Eugene, Or. 2008).

Paul F. Bradshaw, *Reconstructing Early Christian Worship* (SPCK, London 2009), chapters 7–9.

Paul F. Bradshaw and Maxwell E. Johnson, *The Origins of Feasts, Fasts, and Seasons in Early Christianity* (SPCK, London 2011).

11

Daily prayer

Times for prayer

The New Testament implies that at least some early Christians engaged in a regular pattern of daily prayer, since it speaks of the disciples as 'persevering with one accord in the prayer' and 'persevering in . . . the prayers' (Acts 1.14; 2.42, my translation). Similar phrases occur in Acts 6.4, Romans 12.12 and Colossians 4.2. None of these references, however, reveal what this pattern might have been. While there are allusions to specific times of prayer, including the sixth hour (Acts 10.9), night (Acts 12.5, 12), and midnight (Acts 16.25), it is impossible to know whether these were established hours for Christian prayer, or instead were merely occasioned by the particular circumstances being described in the story.

We might expect the first Christians to have continued to observe whatever were the customary Jewish times of daily prayer, but there seems to have been a variety of practice among Jews of the first century: some appear to have prayed twice a day, morning and evening, but others three times a day, either morning, noon and evening, or morning, afternoon (3 p.m.) and evening. Thus, examining Jewish prayer patterns does not help us very much in discovering what the oldest Christian customs were.

The first clear evidence that we have for Christian times of prayer comes from the *Didache* (8.3), which instructs its readers to pray three times a day, although it does not say exactly when those three times were to be: presumably it expected them to know that already. Morning, noon and evening were probably what were intended, as these are mentioned in some third-century sources, although other Christians living in urban settings appear to have preferred to adjust these times to correspond to the principal divisions of the day in the Roman empire that were publicly announced in cities: the third, sixth and ninth hours (9 a.m., 12 noon and 3 p.m.). All these sources add prayer at night to the cycle, and evidence from North Africa reveals the emergence of a conflation of the two methods of threefold daily prayer into a fivefold pattern that would become more or less universally recommended in the fourth century: morning, third hour, sixth hour (= noon), ninth hour and evening.

Eschatological expectation

We might assume that Christians adopted this custom of daily prayer at specific hours simply as the result of the power of tradition: the first converts had prayed at set times when they were Jews, continued to do so when they became Christians, and passed the tradition on to succeeding generations. While this may certainly be part of the reason for the practice, much more meaning was associated with it than that.

The earliest Christians confidently expected the return of Christ and the consummation of the kingdom of God within the immediate future, and believed that they were called to be alert and watchful at all times for that final salvific event. Just as servants were expected to stay awake and watch for the return of their master, so they too were to be vigilant for the return of their Lord (see Mark 13.32–37; Luke 12.35–40). Several New Testament texts suggest that prayer was regarded as the proper mode of this eschatological vigilance. 'Watch and pray that you may not enter into temptation,' says Jesus in the Garden of Gethsemane (Mark 14.38 and parallels); and the same advice is repeated in the epistles: 'persevere in the prayer, being watchful in it with thanksgiving' (Colossians 4.2, my translation); 'praying at all times in the Spirit, and to that end being watchful in all perseverance' (Ephesians 6.18, my translation). The discipline of prayer at regular, fixed times, therefore, was an expression of their constant readiness for the end time, as it also appears to have been among certain Jewish groups of the period.

The offering of life

As time went by, however, and this event failed to happen, the eschatological aspect of daily prayer naturally began to grow dim. Although traces of it can still be seen in Christian writings of the late second and early third centuries, the main justification for maintaining the traditional times of daily prayer has now shifted. Authors of this period continue to repeat St Paul's precept to 'pray constantly' (1 Thessalonians 5.17) as the only absolute rule binding upon Christians, but they tend to see its fulfilment as being in the turning of the whole of one's life into an act of worship offered to God, and the observance of the fixed hours of prayer as a part of this broader obligation.

There are precedents for this way of thinking in the New Testament itself. For example, St Paul urges Christians to 'present your bodies as a living sacrifice, holy and acceptable to God' (Romans 12.1). Moreover, the idea that Christians constituted a priesthood (1 Peter 2.5, 9; Revelation 1.6; 5.10; 20.6) also encouraged them to view the oblation of their life as their priestly sacrifice to God. Christians of the second and third centuries therefore naturally thought of their times of prayer as part of this offering. Thus Tertullian spoke of prayer as 'a spiritual oblation which has abolished the former sacrifices', and Origen saw the daily sacrifices of the Old Testament (described there as 'perpetual': see Exodus 29.38–42; 30.7–8; Numbers 28.3–6) as finding their true fulfilment in the perpetual prayer of Christians.[1]

The 'cathedral' office: the sacrifice of praise

After the Peace of Constantine in the fourth century, Christians began to celebrate publicly certain of the daily hours of prayer which they had previously observed either individually or with their families. The hours generally chosen were the morning and the evening, partly because these were the only ones for which it was practical for most people to gather together (the other times occurred during the working day, and it was not easy or always safe to venture out for prayer at night), and partly because these were now seen as the Christian equivalent of the daily morning and evening sacrifices prescribed by God in the Old Testament. Modern scholars have labelled these public services as the 'cathedral' office, because they

---

[1] Tertullian, *De oratione* 28; Origen, *Homiliae in Numeros* 23.3; *Contra Celsum* 8.17, 21–2.

were understood by those taking part in them as being the Church's sacrifice of praise and priestly intercession for the needs of all. They were therefore composed of two principal elements: hymns and psalms of praise, and prayers for the Church and the world. The hymns and psalms were usually unchanging from day to day. Psalms 148–150 seem to have formed the nucleus of the morning praise everywhere, together with the canticle *Gloria in Excelsis* in the East. The evening seems to have been less fixed, but the hymn *Phos hilaron*, 'Hail gladdening light', was often used in the East as the lamps were lit and thanksgiving offered for the natural light of the day, for the lamplight in the darkness of the night, and for the illumination brought by the light of Christ. Psalm 63, understood to refer to morning, and Psalm 141 with its reference to evening are also found at those hours in many Eastern rites.

The idea that these two occasions constituted the fulfilment of the Old Testament sacrificial law led in the fifth century to the introduction of a regular offering of incense in the services, in accordance with Exodus 30.7–8: 'And Aaron shall burn fragrant incense on [the altar]; every morning when he dresses the lamps he shall burn it, and when Aaron sets up the lamps in the evening, he shall burn it, a perpetual incense before the LORD throughout your generations.'

It will be noted that Bible readings do not appear to have formed a part of these daily hours of prayer. Although the practice was encouraged, it would only have been practical for the few who were educated enough to be able to read and wealthy enough to own a copy of the Scriptures. The rest would have had to rely on what they heard in Sunday services and other occasional gatherings for the ministry of the word (see below, p. 85).

Prayer in the desert: ceaseless meditation

At least from the end of the second century, if not sooner, there were some who regarded the observance of fixed hours of prayer as no more than a second-best way of fulfilling the apostolic injunction to pray without ceasing. The ideal was truly uninterrupted praying. This attitude seems to have been particularly prevalent in Alexandria among those Christians who had come under the influence of the philosophy of Plato and the Stoics, and it was extensively developed by Clement of Alexandria. Although he admitted the necessity of set times of prayer for those not very far advanced in the spiritual life, he stipulated that, for those who would be perfect Christians (or 'Gnostics' as he calls them), prayer was to be a state of continual communion with God:

> During his whole life the Gnostic in every place, even if he be alone by himself, and wherever he has any of those who have exercised the like faith, honours God, that is, acknowledges his gratitude for the knowledge of the way to live ... Holding festival, then, in our whole life, and persuaded that God is altogether on every side present, we cultivate our fields, praising; we sail the sea, hymning ...
>
> Now if some assign fixed hours for prayer – as, for example, the third, and sixth, and ninth – yet the Gnostic prays throughout his whole life, endeavouring by prayer to have fellowship with God. And briefly, having reached to this, he leaves behind him all that is of no service, as having now received the perfection of one who acts by love.[2]

This approach to prayer was appropriated by the ascetics who went out into the deserts of Egypt and Syria in the fourth century, and whose aim was to maintain there as near as possible a ceaseless vigil of prayer, punctuated only by the minimal interruption for food and sleep. Not only did they thus devote more time to actual praying than other Christians, but their concept of prayer was also radically different. They did not see themselves as engaged in offering the Church's sacrifice of praise or praying for the needs of the world, but instead as individuals seeking their own salvation through constant meditation and petition for spiritual growth. Thus the form of the praying was also quite different from that of the 'cathedral' office. Whether praying alone or with others, as the basis for their meditation they mainly used the Old Testament psalms, which they understood as prophecy about Christ, and they alternated the reading of a psalm (or its recitation from memory) with a period of silent prayer. In this manner they gradually worked their way through the whole 150 psalms in order.

---

[2] Clement of Alexandria, *Stromata* 7.7; English translation from William Wilson, *The Writings of Clement of Alexandria*, vol. 2 (T&T Clark, Edinburgh 1872), pp. 431, 432, 435.

Urban monastic prayer: the traditions fused

The fourth century also saw the gradual emergence of especially devout individuals and religious communities who did not make their home in desert regions but remained in towns and cities in close contact with the Church around them. The foundations of their prayer life were the older Christian traditions of praying at least five times each day and again during the night. Inevitably, however, they were influenced both by the spirituality of the desert and also by the practice of the 'cathedral' office around them. As a result, their forms of daily prayer became hybrid in character. They included the selective psalmody of the 'cathedral' services as well as the consecutive recitation of psalms of the desert tradition, and the worshippers thought of themselves both as singing hymns to God and as meditating on the psalms at the same time.

This particular spirituality did not remain restricted to such people alone. Because nearly every important Christian bishop of the second half of the fourth century had lived as a monk at one time or another during his career, the form of spiritual life that they advocated to ordinary lay people was essentially monastic in character. In addition to attendance at the 'cathedral' office every day, therefore, people were encouraged to maintain the other traditional times of prayer individually, and to learn the psalms and recite them frequently, although in practice it seems that few of them did. Nevertheless, in this way, the fusion of early Christian, 'cathedral' and desert traditions passed into the mainstream of Christian spirituality of the succeeding ages.

12

Sunday

New Testament evidence

The New Testament contains only three possible allusions to the early Christian observance of Sunday, and it is not completely clear how each of these should be interpreted. Acts 20.7–12 describes a gathering 'to break bread' that took place 'on the first day of the week' and continued past midnight. But was this the regular occasion for Christian worship every week, or did it take place on that day only because St Paul was about to depart? In 1 Corinthians 16.2, the apostle exhorts his readers to put aside a monetary offering 'on the first day of every week'. But was the day chosen for that activity because the Christians were regularly gathering together for worship then, or for some quite different and unknown reason? Revelation 1.10 states that the author was 'in the Spirit on the Lord's day'. But does the expression 'Lord's day' refer to Sunday, as it seems to do when it occurs again in *Didache* 14 and in Ignatius of Antioch's *Letter to the Magnesians* 9.1, or has it some quite different meaning here, for instance, the eschatological day of the Lord?

Thus, although many scholars believe that Sunday was adopted as a Christian observance as early as the first generation of believers, firm evidence for it does not exist before the end of the first century.

The Christian Sabbath?

Although some Christians have thought that Sunday replaced Saturday as the Sabbath day, most scholars are agreed that, while Jewish Christians may have gone on observing an actual weekly Sabbath, Gentile Christians who adhered to St Paul's view of the Jewish law as no longer binding upon them would have had no interest in keeping any day of the week as a Sabbath. Moreover, while early Christian writings certainly retained the Jewish image of the Sabbath rest, they viewed it as coming at the end of time and not as applying to a day of the week. Sunday was therefore not the Christian Sabbath but the occasion chosen by the early Christians for their weekly gatherings. It did not involve a cessation from work on that day, which in any case would have been impossible for most of them, since it was a regular working day (it was only in the fourth century that the Emperor Constantine made Sunday a public holiday).

Commemoration of the resurrection?

Why did they choose that particular day of the week? Some have thought that it was because, according to the Gospel accounts, Jesus had risen from the dead on 'the first day of the week', and hence Sunday was intended primarily as a commemoration of the resurrection. This certainly seems to be a part of the answer, and it continued to have this function in later centuries. At Jerusalem in the fourth century, for example, there was a special early service every Sunday morning at the site of Christ's tomb during which one of the Gospel accounts of the resurrection was read. This practice subsequently spread to other parts of the world. But other evidence suggests that there was more to the significance of this day than just the remembrance of Christ's resurrection, however important that may have been.

The day of the Eucharist

Jews count each new day as beginning in the evening, not the morning, and hence the most important meal in connection with the Sabbath is that on Friday evening before sunset and the onset of the Sabbath when the lighting of fires and cooking is prohibited because it is considered to be work. Early Jewish Christians, therefore, would doubtless have continued this weekly practice, along with a gathering to study God's word on Saturday mornings, as did other Jews. It is possible that some Gentile Christian communities and even mixed gatherings of Jewish and Gentile believers might initially have adopted the same occasion, but others probably assembled instead for their meal and ministry of the word when the Sabbath was over, after sunset on Saturday, the beginning of the first day of the week. This suggests that the appeals in early Christian writings not to keep the Sabbath but the Lord's day instead were calls to celebrate the eucharistic meal on Saturday evening rather than Friday. As suggested earlier (above, p. 46), the transfer of this to Sunday morning almost certainly happened after the Eucharist was reduced to sharing token amounts of bread and wine.

This explains the remarkable fact that, apart from a single reference in Acts 2.46 to the first Christians meeting day by day to break bread together in their homes (which may well be a bit of idealizing by the author), nearly all other evidence from the first three centuries points to the conclusion that the only days on which Christians regularly celebrated the Eucharist were Sundays, together with saints' days as those emerged in local churches. Even in the fourth century, many churches resisted the extension of the celebration of the Eucharist to other days. Churches in the East added a Saturday celebration to the Sunday, almost certainly building on a continuing Jewish-Christian tradition from earliest times of having a service of the word on that day. But while some churches also turned the regular Wednesday and Friday services of the word (see below, pp. 86–7) into full celebrations of the Eucharist as well, others did not, and still others adopted a compromise, in which communion was given at those services, but with bread and wine consecrated at the Sunday Eucharist. While Western Christians did gradually move towards celebrating the Eucharist on any day of the week, Eastern Christians have continued to adhere to the tradition of a full celebration only on Saturdays, Sundays and other holy days.

Sunday was thus the day for the manifestation, or epiphany, of the Church. During the rest of the week the Church was dispersed and hidden, as its individual members went about their life and work in different places. But on Sunday the Church came together and revealed itself in the celebration of the Eucharist, with each member occupying his or her proper place in the assembly.

The Lord's day

Sunday was not just the occasion for a commemoration of a past event – the resurrection – but the celebration of a present experience – communion with the risen Christ. But it also had a strong orientation towards the future as well. Not only did the Eucharist itself have an eschatological dimension, symbolizing the messianic banquet at the end of time, but the chief title given to the day by early Christians, the Lord's day, also expressed that same vision. Old Testament prophets had used a similar expression, 'the day of the Lord', to refer to the end of time, and so the Christian term implies the notion that Sunday was a symbolic anticipation of the age to come when Christ would be Lord of all, just as he was already Lord for believers. For the same reason, both kneeling for prayer and fasting were forbidden on this day in the early Church, as they were thought incompatible with its joyful character as a foretaste of the kingdom of God.

The eighth day

Sunday was also known by some Christians as 'the eighth day'. Since in Jewish thought the number seven symbolized perfection, the concept of an eighth day obviously signified something greater still. Because according to Psalm 90.4 a thousand years was like a single day in the sight of the Lord, the Christians imagined that this world would last for six days (i.e. six thousand years), to be followed by a seventh day, a thousand years when Jesus would reign as Messiah, and then an eighth day, a final golden age that would last for ever. Hence, in giving the same title to Sunday, they were envisaging it as a symbolic foretaste of that eschatological time to which they looked forward in hope.

Wednesday and Friday

Didache 8.1 directed Christians not to fast on Mondays and Thursdays (the regular Jewish fast-days) but on Wednesdays and Fridays, and this custom continued to be widely observed in later centuries, with regular services of the word also taking place at the ninth hour (about 3 p.m.) on these days. It has traditionally been assumed that Christians made this change in order to differentiate their practices more clearly from those of the Jews and merely picked these days at random. However, this assumption did not take into account how deeply rooted liturgical customs tend to be, and how unlikely random change would be. More recent scholars have concluded, therefore, that the first Christian converts may have been influenced in their choice by the solar calendar in use among the Essene Jewish community at

Qumran, in which Wednesday and Friday had a certain prominence, even though these days were not marked by fasting or by any special liturgical assemblies at Qumran so far as we are aware. The substitution of the ninth hour instead of the morning for a service of the word, as on the Jewish fast-days, appears to have been made in order to commemorate the death of Jesus at that hour (Matthew 27.46–50; Mark 15.34–37; Luke 23.44–46).

13

Easter and Pentecost

Early Christian sources reveal two quite distinct modes of celebrating Easter. The one that ultimately became universal was to keep the feast on the Sunday following the Jewish Passover and to focus its celebration upon the resurrection of Jesus Christ from the dead, which – according to the four canonical Gospels – had taken place on the first day of the week. The other ancient form of the celebration is attested chiefly in second-century sources deriving from Asia Minor. This tradition makes Easter a memorial of the death of Jesus, and situates the feast instead at the time of the Jewish Passover itself, during the night from 14 to 15 Nisan. Because of their attachment to the fourteenth day of the Jewish month, those who followed this custom were called 'Quartodecimans' (i.e. 'fourteeners') by other Christians.

The traditional consensus of scholars used to be that the Sunday celebration was the older of the two (perhaps even going as far back as the apostolic age itself, even though it is only explicitly attested from the second century onwards) and was the one observed by the mainstream of the Christian tradition. The Quartodeciman custom was judged to be no more than a second-century local aberration from this norm, brought about by an apparently common tendency among some early Christians to 'Judaize', a practice already criticized by St Paul in the first century (see, for example, the Letter to the Galatians).

On the other hand, more recently some scholars have claimed that the Quartodeciman practice began at a much earlier date as a Jewish-Christian adaptation of the Passover festival. Others have gone further still and argued that the celebration of Easter on a Sunday was a considerably later development than is often supposed – that it was not adopted at Rome until about 165, although it may have emerged in Alexandria and Jerusalem somewhat earlier. Prior to this time, these churches would have known no annual Easter observance at all. If this theory is correct, as it seems to be, then it effectively reverses the older consensus, so that Quartodecimanism is not some local aberration from a supposed normative practice dating from apostolic times, but is instead the oldest form of the Easter celebration.

It is not difficult to understand how leaders of early Christian communities that did not at first observe an annual commemoration of Christ's death and resurrection might have desired to adopt the practice they saw among the Quartodecimans. Nor is it hard to appreciate why they would have preferred to locate this innovation on the Sunday immediately following the Passover rather than on the actual feast itself: since Sunday was already the occasion of their regular weekly celebration of the paschal mystery, it would obviously be easier to develop that existing liturgical day than to persuade congregations to embrace a completely new event.

The meaning of the feast

The above hypothesis certainly helps to explain several somewhat puzzling features of the early Christian observance of Easter, and not least the meaning that was given to it. For not only in Quartodeciman circles but also at first among those who kept the feast on Sunday, the original focus of the celebration was not on the resurrection of Christ but rather on 'Christ, the Passover lamb, sacrificed for us'. While this seems a perfectly natural direction for a feast situated on the Jewish Passover to have taken, it appears to be a less obvious path for the Sunday celebration, if it were not originally derived from the Quartodeciman custom.

The image of Christ as the Passover lamb is found in 1 Corinthians 5.7, and also underlies John's Gospel. There Jesus is identified as 'the Lamb of God' near the beginning (1.36) and is said to have died on the cross on the day of the preparation of the Passover (i.e. 14 Nisan) at the hour when the lambs for the feast were being slaughtered (19.14ff.). In addition, the soldiers are said to have refrained from breaking the legs of the dead Jesus in order that the Scripture requiring no bone of the Passover lamb to be broken (19.32–36; cf. Exodus 12.46; Numbers 9.12) might be fulfilled.

That this theme was central to the Quartodecimans' celebration can be seen not merely from the date on which Easter took place, but also from the emphasis on the suffering and death of Christ found in their writings. Indeed, they even claimed that the name of the feast, Pascha (which in reality is simply a transliteration of the

Aramaic form of the Hebrew *pesach*, meaning Passover), was derived from the Greek verb *paschein*, 'to suffer'. Precisely the same interpretation and theology of the feast occur in the writings of those early Christians who kept Easter on Sunday.

At the end of the second century in Alexandria, however, we encounter a different understanding of the feast, one that focused upon 'passage' rather than 'passion' – the passage from death to life. Clement of Alexandria describes the Passover as humanity's passage 'from all trouble and all objects of sense' (*Stromata* 2.11.51.2); and Origen in the middle of the third century explains this interpretation more fully: most Christians think that 'the Pascha is named Pascha from the passion of the Savior. However, the feast in question is not called precisely Pascha by the Hebrews, but *phas[h]* . . . Translated it means "passage." Since it is on this feast that the people goes forth from Egypt, it is logical to call it *phas[h]*, that is, "passage".'[1]

Fourth-century Alexandrian Christians tended to combine the two interpretations. Although this change of focus may in part be simply the result of a more accurate exegesis of the Hebrew Scriptures, it is also in line with the general tendency among Alexandrian theologians to allegorize and de-historicize the Christian mysteries. We may also add the influence that would have been exercised by the day on which the feast occurred: Sundays throughout the year were primarily associated with the resurrection of Christ to new life rather than with his death. Moreover, evidence from both Egypt and Syria in the third century reveals the beginnings of a trend to view the Easter observance as a *triduum*, a three-day celebration of the transition from death to resurrection. But in order to understand this development, we must first take a look at the origins of the paschal fast.

The paschal fast and the *triduum*

The limited evidence that exists for the form of the Quartodeciman observance suggests that the period of fasting which in Jewish tradition preceded the eating of the Passover meal at nightfall on 14 Nisan was extended by the Christians into a vigil during the night, so that their celebration of the feast with a eucharistic meal only began after

---

[1] *On the Pascha* 1; English translation from Raniero Cantalamessa, *Easter in the Early Church* (Liturgical Press, Collegeville 1993), p. 53.

the Jewish festivities were over. The Sunday celebration also included a preceding day of fasting and a night vigil culminating in the celebration of the Eucharist. Once again, these two elements are easier to comprehend when understood as appropriations from the Quartodeciman practice. For there does not seem to be anything intrinsic to the nature of the Sunday celebration to have given rise either to a day of fasting or to a vigil. Moreover, most early Christian communities regarded all Saturdays, like Sundays, as inappropriate for fasting – no doubt a vestige of respect for the Sabbath that had been inherited from Judaism – and thus the introduction of a fast on a Saturday would have constituted a significant break with tradition which could not have been done lightly.

It was not long, however, before the Saturday fast became extended in some Christian communities. As we have seen, it was already a well established tradition for Christians to keep every Wednesday and Friday throughout the year as days of fasting, and so some churches began to join the regular Friday fast and the Saturday paschal fast together to create a continuous two-day preparatory fast before the Easter festival. Some Christians in Egypt and Syria went even further and created a six-day fast from Monday until the end of the Saturday vigil. The Syrian church order known as the *Didascalia Apostolorum* gives a detailed explanation of the practice. This document maintains that Judas was paid for his betrayal 'on the tenth day of the month, on the Monday' (5.17.8), and so it was as though Jesus had already been seized on that day, in fulfilment of the Old Testament requirement to take a lamb on the tenth day of the month and keep it until the fourteenth (Exodus 12.3, 6). It then continues:

> Therefore you shall fast during the days of the Pascha from the tenth, which is a Monday; and you shall sustain yourselves with bread and salt and water only, at the ninth hour, until the Thursday. But on the Friday and on the Saturday fast completely, and do not taste anything. You shall come together and watch and keep vigil all the night with prayers and intercessions, and with reading of the Prophets, and with the Gospels and with Psalms, and fear and trembling, and with earnest supplication, until the third hour in the night after the Saturday; and then break your fasts.[2]

---

[2] 5.18.1–5.19.1 (Sebastian Brock and Michael Vasey, *The Liturgical Portions of the Didascalia* (Grove Books, Nottingham 1982), p. 28).

This passage is interesting in several respects. First, we may note that because the term Pascha is understood to refer to the passion of Christ, it is used to denote the period of the memorial of Christ's suffering and death, and not the celebration of his resurrection, as is also the case in other early sources: strictly speaking, the Pascha ends at the conclusion of the fast and vigil. Second, the biblical prescriptions about the timing of the Passover have been adapted to fit a quite different chronology, which may possibly be an indication that this section of the text has Quartodeciman roots. Third, this chronology would clearly make Friday the day on which Christ died (even though it does not seem as yet to be marked by any special liturgical observance), and therefore begin to point the Easter vigil in the direction of being a memorial more of the resurrection than of the death of Christ or of the whole paschal mystery. This transition of meaning is in fact made clear by another reference to the end of the vigil later in the text: 'after which eat and enjoy yourselves, and rejoice and be glad, because Christ, the pledge of our own resurrection, is risen'.[3] Finally, although the church order does prescribe six days of fasting, a distinction is still maintained between the older two-day fast and the other days of the week, and this is also emphasized in other parts of the document: 'Especially incumbent on you therefore is the fast of the Friday and Saturday...Fast then on the Friday, because on that day the People killed themselves in crucifying our Saviour; and on the Saturday as well, because it is the sleep of the Lord; for it is a day which ought especially to be kept with fasting.'[4]

A similar development can also be seen in the Egyptian sources. In the passage from Clement of Alexandria cited above as the earliest evidence for the understanding of the feast as 'passage', he too spoke of it as having begun 'on the tenth day'; and Origen clearly viewed the paschal events as extending over three days, in fulfilment of Hosea 6.2, even if they were not yet liturgically celebrated in this way: 'Now listen to what the prophet says: "God will revive us after two days, and on the third day we shall rise and live in his sight." For us the first day is the passion of the Savior; the

---

[3] 5.19.7 (Brock and Vasey, *Liturgical Portions of the Didascalia*, p. 28).

[4] 5.19.6, 9–10 (Brock and Vasey, *Liturgical Portions of the Didascalia*, p. 28).

second on which he descended into hell; and the third, the day of resurrection.'[5]

In the light of all this, it is not surprising to find in sources from the late fourth century the emergence of the liturgical observance of Good Friday as the memorial of Christ's death, with Easter itself now being regarded as essentially the celebration of his resurrection. To this was added Holy Saturday as the commemoration of his burial and/or descent into Hell. This development seems to have begun at Jerusalem itself in connection with the sacred sites associated with the passion and resurrection, and spread slowly from there to other parts of the Church.

Pentecost

A number of sources at the end of the second century indicate the existence of a 50-day season following Easter. Called Pentecost, it was regarded as a time of rejoicing, and every day was treated in the same way as Sunday, that is, with no kneeling for prayer or fasting. Since the Jewish feast of Pentecost was celebrated only on the fiftieth day after the Passover, and did not involve any special treatment of the intervening period, this season appears to be a purely Christian innovation, intended to extend the celebration of Easter. At first no particular emphasis appears to have been placed on the fiftieth day itself by Christians, but in the fourth century we find that day being celebrated as a commemoration of the gift of the Holy Spirit, in accordance with Acts 2. In some places the celebration of the day also included the Ascension of Christ, but towards the end of the century a separate feast of the Ascension on the fortieth day (Acts 1.3) emerged in a number of places and became almost universal early in the fifth century. Thus the original unity of the 50-day season was gradually broken down, and regular fasting resumed after the fortieth day, or in some places even before it.

---

[5] *Homiliae in Exodum* 5.2; English translation from Cantalamessa, *Easter in the Early Church*, p. 55.

14

Christmas, Epiphany and Lent

No local church at first observed both 25 December and 6 January as festivals. The observance of 6 January as the manifestation of Christ (Epiphany or Theophany) seems to be the older of the two, perhaps dating from the third century, and is found in many places, both East and West, in the fourth century. The celebration of the nativity of Jesus on 25 December, on the other hand, appears to have originated in Rome (which did not then keep 6 January) probably early in the fourth century. It is first mentioned in what is known as the Roman Chronograph of 354, which gives a list of significant days in the year for the city of Rome probably drawn up nearly 20 years earlier, in 336.

Two competing theories

What is not clear is why these two particular dates were chosen as festivals. Two main theories have been put forward by modern scholars to account for the choice. One, termed the 'history of religions' hypothesis, asserts that they had been selected because they were the occasion of pagan winter solstice celebrations in different calendars in use in the ancient world, and Christian leaders wanted to draw people away from such festivities and offer a Christian counter-attraction to them. Certainly, 25 December was the date assigned to the solstice in the Julian calendar and also of a very popular pagan feast at Rome, established by the emperor Aurelian in 274 to celebrate the *dies natalis solis invicti*, the birthday of the invincible sun. We also know that certain other Christian holy days originally emerged precisely as alternatives to pagan celebrations already held on those dates: 1 January, for example, became a Christian day of penitence in several places, and then later a feast of Mary at Rome, because pagans were keeping the date as a festival of the god Janus.

Unfortunately, however, no such correlation really exists for 6 January in other parts of the world. At one time it was thought that the eastern provinces of the Roman empire observed the date as the winter solstice in accordance with the ancient calendar of Amenemhet I of Thebes, and the Christian feast was established to coincide with that occasion. However, it has since been established that there never was a calendar of Amenemhet I; that 6 January was nowhere thought to be the winter solstice; and that there is no strong evidence that it was once the occasion of a widespread pagan festival.

The alternative theory, generally known as the 'calculation' hypothesis, claims that the dates were arrived at as the result of ancient attempts to work out the exact day in the year on which Jesus had been born. It is true that there is evidence from at least the end of the second century onwards of individuals trying to work out the precise date of both Jesus' death and birth, but the weakness of the theory is that none of them seem to have suggested 25 December for the birth, although 25 March was one of the possibilities for his death. Scholars who advocate this hypothesis, therefore, have pointed out that because great figures in the ancient world were believed to have lived for an exact number of years, the date of their death was often thought to have been the same as that on which they were born. They argue that in Jesus' case it was the date of his conception that was equated with the date of his death, with his birth nine months later, in the West on 25 December and in the East on 6 January, because his death was there reckoned to have been on 6 April. However, the greatest weakness of this hypothesis is that there is a complete lack of evidence to show why uniquely in Jesus' case the date of his conception rather than his birth might have been chosen. Thus, neither theory can claim to have definitively established the reason for the dates of the two feasts.

25 December

Whatever the reason for the selection of 25 December, it is important to note that the day came to be thought of at Rome as more than just a commemoration of the birthday of Jesus. For instance, the oldest Gospel readings associated with the feast there were not only Luke's story of the birth of Jesus but also the beginning of the Gospel of John, with its assertion that 'the Word became flesh and dwelt among us' (1.14). In other words, what was being celebrated was not just the historical event of the nativity, but belief in the reality of the incarnation of the Son of God: hence there was a strong doctrinal or apologetic purpose shaping the festival and not merely a popular piety. Some scholars have suggested that this may account at least in part for its eventual adoption elsewhere. Even though the Arian heresy had already been condemned at the Council of Nicaea in 325, the fourth century continued to be a period of intense debate about the nature of the person of Christ and so a festival that affirmed his divinity would have had a certain attraction. Others, however, have argued the opposite: that a celebration of the birth of the infant Jesus might have been seen as more supportive of the Arian cause, and that may be why its diffusion happened only quite slowly. For although the festival did spread to North Africa (which, like Rome, probably also did not keep 6 January at this time) by the middle of the fourth century, it was not until the second half of the century that it was adopted in places where 6 January was already being kept. It did not reach Jerusalem or Egypt until the fifth century, and it was never accepted at all in Armenia.

6 January

As early as the late second or early third century among some Christians in Egypt, 6 January was associated with both the birth and the baptism of Jesus, apparently understood as constituting a single reality. This same combination of themes as expressing the manifestation of Christ's divinity seems to have persisted when the celebration of this day spread to other parts of the East, with the miracle at Cana in Galilee (John 2.1–11) often being added as a further aspect of that revelation. However, because emphasis on Christ's baptism as his birth or 'beginning' obviously carried with it the unwanted implication of an Adoptionist Christology (that is, that the human Jesus was only 'adopted' as God's son at some point after his birth), fourth-century doctrinal controversies naturally encouraged the separation of the themes, with the addition of 25 December to the calendar focusing on the birth alone, and 6 January on the baptism and wedding at Cana. Jerusalem appears to have been an exception to this, making 6 January a commemoration of the nativity event instead (including the visit of the Magi, Matthew 2.1–12) and not adopting 25 December until some time later. Conversely, the addition of 6 January as a festival in Rome and North Africa resulted in the feast there being centred on the visit of the Magi as marking Christ's manifestation, with the commemoration of Jesus' baptism and the wedding at Cana being relegated to subsequent and subordinate days in the calendar.

Lent

The origins of this season appear to lie in Egypt, where at least from the beginning of the fourth century if not earlier, there was a 40-day fast, kept in imitation of Jesus' 40-day fast in the wilderness after his baptism (Matthew 4.1–11; Mark 1.12–13; Luke 4.1–13). This annual period of fasting seems to have occurred immediately after 6 January, which the Egyptian Church observed as the commemoration of the baptism of Jesus. It also appears to have been used as the time of fasting before the baptism of new converts, which consequently took place at the close of the 40-day period, and as the final period of penitential fasting for serious sinners before they were allowed to return to participation in the community's eucharistic worship.

Later in the fourth century we find the churches in other parts of the world also observing a similar 40-day season of fasting, which they doubtless adopted from the Egyptian custom. However, they did not locate it following 6 January but instead immediately before their pre-Easter fast, where at least some of them – notably Rome and North Africa – were already accustomed to hold a pre-baptismal fast in preparation for baptism at Easter.[1] This meant that for those churches which observed only two days of fasting (Friday and Saturday) before the festival, the Lenten season began on the Sunday six weeks before Easter and ended on the Thursday immediately prior to Easter. For the churches of the East, which kept six days of fasting before Easter (from Monday to Saturday), Lent began on the Monday of the seventh week before Easter and ended on the Friday nine days before Easter, with the following Saturday and Sunday as a festal intermission between the two fasts. The church at Alexandria was an

---

[1] For Easter baptism, see above, pp. 17–18, 25; for the pre-Easter fast, see pp. 90–1.

exception to this Eastern custom. It apparently made the transition to the pre-Easter position somewhat later than the rest and, when it did so, set its beginning only six weeks before Easter, thus overlapping the six-day pre-Easter fast that it had formerly observed.

Because no church ever fasted on Sundays, and many churches did not fast on Saturdays either (with the sole exception of the Saturday immediately before Easter), the 40-day season always contained fewer than 40 days of actual fasting. Gradually, therefore, various churches began to move its beginning backwards so as to extend its length and produce a full 40 days of fasting.

15

Saints' days

As we have seen, prior to the fourth century the only annual festival that was universally observed was Easter, with its preparatory fast beforehand and its 50-day celebration afterwards. The calendars of the various churches would have been filled out with the commemoration of one or more local martyrs on the anniversary of the date on which they had died, but usually termed by early Christians as their 'birthday' (in Latin, *natale*). The choice of this particular word indicates their conviction that for those who had suffered and died for the Christian faith, death was the gateway to a new beginning, life eternal in heaven with Christ, in whose suffering they had participated. Unlike other Christians, who were thought to sleep in death until the time of the return of Christ in glory, martyrs were believed to be accorded immediate admittance to the presence of God.

Our earliest reference to this custom comes from an account of the martyrdom of Polycarp of Smyrna in the middle of the second century, although the account itself may have been composed rather later, in the third century. This tells us that, after he had been burned to death, 'thus at last taking up his bones, being more precious than jewels and finer than gold, we put them where it was fitting. Assembling there as we can, the Lord will grant us to celebrate the birthday of his martyrdom with joy and gladness, both in memory of those who have already striven, and for the practice and preparation of those who are to do so.'[1]

It is important to notice that this early custom was intensely *local*. Churches usually only celebrated the festivals of their own martyrs, and not those of other localities. Moreover, the celebration was held not in the house or other building where the local church normally met, but in the very place where the remains of the martyr were

---

[1] *Martyrdom of Polycarp* 18.2–3.

interred. The basis for this custom was the funerary meals of contemporary Greek and Roman society, which were held at the tomb on the deceased person's birthday. In the fourth century Christians began to erect church buildings over the place of burial in which to hold their celebrations, and the sites often became the objects of popular pilgrimage.

It is also important to observe the significance attached to the physical remains of the martyr, as is evidenced by the extract above from the account of the martyrdom of Polycarp. From the beginning, the cult of the martyrs was closely related to such relics, and this explains in large part why celebrations were slow to spread from one local church community to another: other churches did not possess the remains of the martyr around which to organize a cult. It was only later, in the second half of the fourth century, that the practice began of often moving the mortal remains of martyrs from the original place of burial to a more suitable location in an existing church, especially when the tomb was a considerable distance away from the city itself. Previously, such an action would have been thought sacrilegious in the pagan society of the period. Yet now this development facilitated the removal of individual relics of the martyr – a small bone, for example – from the rest of the body and transporting it to another city, where it could form the basis of a cult there. In this way, churches gradually began to add to their own calendars festivals of martyrs from other places.

The need for relics also helps to explain why the cult of New Testament saints was generally somewhat slow in developing, since the site of their place of burial was usually at first unknown, and why, when this cult did begin, it was not in the West but in the East, as relics gradually began to be 'found' there. Visits by pilgrims to the Holy Land in the fourth century encouraged this practice, as well as the veneration of Old Testament figures whose tombs were regular stopping-places on the itineraries, although this latter cult did not spread much outside the Eastern churches.

The fourth century also saw the beginnings of the extension of the concept of saints from martyrs alone to other holy men and women. Since the persecution of Christians had now ceased, forms of ascetic life were thought of as constituting a spiritual martyrdom. The noble events of the lives of outstanding ascetic figures were recorded by their disciples, and a cult established around them. Similarly, bishops often initiated the cult of an illustrious predecessor in their episcopal office, no doubt often in the hope that something similar would be done for them when they eventually died.

We need to bear in mind that what was going on in all this was not the *worship* of the saints themselves. Early Christian theologians were insistent that true worship belonged to God alone, but the saints were to be honoured as faithful disciples of Christ. Moreover, just as Christians might ask especially holy people to pray to God on their behalf during their lifetime, so they continued to ask the saints to intercede for them after death, when those men and women were thought to be in the immediate presence of God and so in a position to be effective advocates for the living.

Index

Addai and Mari, Anaphora of 60, 68
adherence, act of 13, 14, 25, 29;
  see also faith, profession of
agape 43–4
Alexandria 14, 21, 63, 80–1, 88, 90,
  92, 97
Ambrose of Milan 24–5, 27, 29–32,
  58, 61
Amen 47, 48, 51, 61, 71–2
Amenemhet I of Thebes 95
anamnesis 49, 52, 54; see also
  remembrance
anointing 5–6, 8, 10–12, 13, 21, 25,
  27–32, 37–8; see also chrism
Antioch 13, 14, 24, 26, 57, 83
Apostolic Tradition 17–20, 22, 26–7,
  29, 30, 34, 44, 45, 53–4, 59, 65,
  66
Arian 71, 96
Armenia 11, 12, 96
Ascension 93
Augustine of Hippo 33–6
Aurelian 94

baptism 1–38, 48, 97; of infants 21,
  33–8; of Jesus 3, 5, 8, 12, 96–7
Basil of Caesarea 60, 71
bishop(s) 10–11, 16, 19, 22, 24, 27,
  30, 37–8, 52, 53, 60, 61, 66–7, 69,
  82, 100

catechumen/catechumenate 4, 14, 18,
  23, 26–7, 37
'cathedral' office 79–82
chrism 14, 21, 28, 30, 31, 38
Christmas 94–7
Christological/Christology 54, 58, 96
Clement of Alexandria 81, 90, 92
communion 13, 31, 37, 42, 43, 48,
  51, 53, 54, 57, 62, 70–4

'confirmation', rite of 5–6, 37–8
consecration 58–61
Constantine 70, 79, 84
Constantinople 13
conversion 23–4, 36, 70
Cornelius, Bishop of Rome 16
Creed 14, 20, 37
Cyprian of Carthage 22, 33, 34, 36,
  37, 45, 66–7
Cyril of Alexandria 14
Cyril of Jerusalem 24–5, 28, 31, 58,
  60, 67, 68, 71

deacons 10–11, 47, 53, 74
Decentius of Gubbio 38
Didache 9–10, 12, 19, 45, 50–1, 52,
  53, 56, 64, 77, 83, 86
Didascalia Apostolorum 10–13, 18,
  21, 30, 91

Easter 14, 17–18, 25, 26, 37, 88–93,
  97–8, 99
Egypt 13–14, 25, 29, 49, 52, 55, 59,
  62, 81, 90–2, 96, 97
'eighth day' 86
epiclesis 49, 51, 52, 54, 59–60, 61, 74
Epiphany, feast of 14, 25, 94–7
eschatological 7, 42, 51, 78, 83, 85, 86
Essene 3, 86
Eucharist 16, 22, 24, 25, 31, 39–74,
  84–5, 90–1
Eusebius 16
exorcism 18, 26–8, 37

faith, profession of 4–5, 13, 14, 18,
  20–1, 24, 25, 29, 34–5, 36; see also
  adherence, act of
fasting 9, 14, 15–16, 18, 25, 26, 86–7,
  90–3, 97–8, 99
foot-washing 6, 25, 30

Index

forgiveness 7, 15, 21, 23, 68
Friday 84–5, 86–7, 91–3, 97

Gentile 4, 5, 52, 83–4
Gloria in Excelsis 80
godparent 35, 36
Gregory of Nazianzus 33, 67

hand(s), imposition of 5–6, 10–11,
    16, 19, 20, 22, 30, 32, 37–8, 53
Hippolytus 17, 18, 53
Holy Spirit 5, 7, 8, 9–10, 11–12,
    15–16, 18–22, 27, 29, 30–2, 38,
    52, 53–4, 59–61, 74, 93
hymn 48, 55, 72, 80, 82

Ignatius of Antioch 57, 83
incarnation 96
incense 52, 63, 80
Innocent I 38
instruction, pre-baptismal 4, 9, 13,
    14, 16, 18, 24, 26, 27
intercession 47, 53, 55, 68–9, 80,
    91, 101
Irenaeus of Lyons 59, 65

James, Liturgy of St 72
Jerusalem 5, 24, 26, 29, 31–2, 43, 44,
    58, 60, 62, 63, 67, 68, 71, 84, 88,
    93, 96
Jewish 3, 4, 42, 44, 45, 47, 49–52, 55,
    63, 77, 78, 83–7, 88–91, 93
John the Baptist 3, 5, 18
John Chrysostom 13, 14, 24–5,
    28–32, 60, 67, 70–3
Justin Martyr 7, 15–17, 44, 47–8, 51,
    56–8, 64, 66

kiss 15–16, 25, 27, 31, 48
kneeling 18, 86, 93

Last Supper 41–4, 53, 54, 65, 66
Lent 14, 25–7, 37, 97–8
Logos 58–9
Lord's day 18, 64, 83, 85–6
Lord's Prayer 37

martyrs 52, 68, 99–100
Messiah/messianic 3, 8, 11–12, 43, 86
milk and honey 22
monastic prayer 82
mystagogy 24

narrative of institution 54, 61, 66
New Testament 1, 3–6, 8, 16, 24, 26,
    32, 33, 41, 45, 46, 47, 50, 56, 63,
    65, 77–9, 83, 100
Nicaea 55, 96
North Africa 1, 6, 14, 16, 17–22,
    25, 26, 33, 35, 38, 78, 96, 97
Novatian 16, 37

Old Testament 22, 26, 31, 42, 49, 56,
    64–5, 68, 79–80, 81, 86, 91, 100
Origen 21, 36, 79, 90, 92
original sin 36

pagan 12, 16, 23, 26, 28, 45, 47,
    94–5, 100
Pascha 89–92
Passover 17, 41–2, 62, 65, 88–90,
    92, 93
Paul, Acts of 9
Pelagius 35
Pentecost 6, 18, 93
persecution 23, 100
Philo of Alexandria 63
Polycarp of Smyrna 99, 100
preaching 24, 47–8, 71–4
presbyters 11, 37–8, 53
priest/priesthood 8, 10–11, 21,
    29–31, 38, 61, 65–7, 73, 79–80
prophets: Christian 51; Old Testament
    8, 15, 47, 52, 64, 68, 86, 91, 92
psalms 80–2, 91

Quartodeciman 88–92
Qumran 3, 45, 63, 87

remembrance 49–50, 54, 62, 65–7, 84
renunciation of evil 13, 19, 25, 29
Rome/Roman 6, 14, 15–18, 25–7,
    31, 35, 37–8, 47, 88, 94–7

Index

Sabbath 47, 83–5, 91
sacrifice 42, 45, 52, 56, 59, 62–9,
71, 79–81, 89
saints' days 85, 99–101
Sarapion, Sacramentary of 14, 59, 60
scrutiny (baptismal) 14, 18
seal/sealing (baptismal) 3, 6–8, 11,
13, 16, 21, 22, 24, 25, 27, 28,
30–2, 37–8
Strasbourg Papyrus 52–5, 64, 68
Sunday 26, 37, 47, 57, 80, 83–6,
88–91, 93, 97–8
synagogue 47–8, 55
Syria/Syrian 1, 4, 6, 9–14, 16, 18, 19,
21, 22, 25, 28–9, 31–2, 53, 60, 68,
81, 90, 91

Temple 42, 62, 63
Tertullian 17–22, 29, 30–1, 33, 57,
79
Thecla 9
Theodore of Mopsuestia 13, 24–5,
28, 31–2, 60, 71, 74
Thomas, Acts of 11
triduum 90–3
Trinity/trinitarian 9, 14, 16, 20–1, 25,
28–31, 54, 59

vigil 18, 81, 90–2

Wednesday 85, 86–7, 91
word (ministry of) 13, 47–8, 80,
84–5, 86